MoviesDoorToDoor.com

How Accounting Helped Make the Difference

Mark S. Beasley

Frank A. Buckless

North Carolina State University

Prentice Hall

Upper Saddle River, New Jerse

D1416609

Dedicated to

Beth, Johnson, Ann Archer, and Will Beasley

Garrett, Cara, and Hayley Buckless

Acquisitions Editor: Thomas Sigel
Editor-in-Chief: P. J. Boardman
Editorial Assistant: Fran Toepfer
Executive Marketing Manager: Beth Toland
Marketing Assistant: Brian Rappelfeld
Managing Editor: John Roberts
Associate Director, Manufacturing: Vincent Scelta
Production Manager: Arnold Vila
Manufacturing Buyer: Michelle Klein
Design Manager: Patricia Smythe
Cover Design: Janet Slowik
Cover Illustration: John Sagan
Printer/Binder: Maple-Vail

Pearson Education LTD.
Pearson Education Australia PTY, Limited
Pearson Education Singapore, Pte. Ltd
Pearson Education North Asia Ltd
Pearson Education, Canada, Ltd
Pearson Educación de Mexico, S.A. de C.V.
Pearson Education–Japan
Pearson Education Malaysia, Pte. Ltd

10 9 8 7 6 5 4
ISBN 0-13-061047-X

Contents

Preface

One of the greatest challenges when teaching most business courses is helping students see the relevance and value of the course content for their future business careers. While students frequently share dreams of becoming an entrepreneur, they often struggle with understanding how course materials will ever personally affect them.

This concern is particularly relevant when teaching introductory courses in accounting. At most institutions, the majority of students enrolled in the introductory course are majoring in fields other than accounting. Many of these students approach the course with some trepidation and doubt whether the material will have much long-term benefit for them personally. Furthermore, the lack of a solid understanding of business concepts often causes students to struggle with mastering the technical accounting content because they are unable to recognize how the accounting concepts and issues affect major business decisions.

The purpose of *MoviesDoorToDoor.com: How Accounting Helped Make the Difference* is to present accounting and business concepts in a logical order consistent with the way business owners and managers face them in the business world. This book features in a fictional story format three young entrepreneurs, Brad, Courtney and John, who must make numerous business decisions as they create and grow a start-up company. While none of the business founders has much accounting training or experience, they quickly realize that many of their business decisions must be based on solid accounting information. The story describes how they use that information when encountering both trials and triumphs while starting a traditional "brick and mortar" business that has an Internet-based component in the uncertain technology economy.

This book is divided into twelve short chapters that deal with various business decisions made by Brad, Courtney and John as their business unfolds. Rather than address the issues in the order they are presented on the balance sheet, much like many traditional textbooks for introductory accounting do, this book introduces accounting and other business activities in a chronological order most consistent with what business owners would actually face when creating and growing a business. We believe that presenting accounting concepts in a story format that intertwines both personal and business issues will motivate student interest in the content of the introductory course in accounting, thus increasing their learning. Discussion questions at the end of each chapter are designed to stimulate class discussion on related accounting and business concepts.

This book is intended to be used as a supplemental reading in an introductory accounting course, at the undergraduate or MBA levels. There are a couple of approaches instructors can take to integrate this with other course materials. One approach would be to assign the reading of the book early in the semester or quarter to give students an overview of the business context of how accounting is used. Relevant chapter materials can be referenced throughout the semester or quarter as the concepts are introduced in class. Another approach would be to spread the reading of each of the chapters evenly over the semester or quarter period, requiring only a few minutes of reading each week. Instructors would take a few moments during class periods to link the concepts to the textbook material. Under either approach, the discussion questions, whether answered individually or in groups, can be used to stimulate rich class discussions.

Because this book also presents issues faced when developing and creating a new business, the use of *MoviesDoorToDoor.com: How Accounting Helped Make the Difference* can also be used in an introductory business course, a course on small businesses, or an entrepreneurial-focused class. In addition, this book may be an effective resource for executive education or other corporate programs focused on training non-accounting or non-business professionals.

The company and characters presented in *MoviesDoorToDoor.com: How Accounting Helped Make the Difference* are purely fictional and are not intended to portray real persons, organizations or events. Also, the book is not intended to present all aspects of a start-up business. However, we have attempted to make the book representative of relevant personalities and experiences one might expect to encounter when starting a new business.

Finally, we would like to thank Eric Blazer of Millersville University, Mary Ann M. Prater of Clemson University and Dan Stone of the University of Kentucky for providing content and instructional feedback related to this project. We are also grateful to Jason Danforth, a student at the University of North Carolina at Chapel Hill, for providing extensive feedback to ensure the book increased student interest and learning in accounting and business. And, we appreciate the helpful insights of Andrea Buckless and Craig Welch, both non-accounting educators, and Beth Beasley, a former bank commercial loan officer. We especially thank Thomas Sigel, Executive Editor, of Prentice Hall who embraced this project with enthusiasm. We also thank other members of the Prentice Hall team including Beth Toland, Laura Rogers, and John Roberts for their hard work. Most importantly, we are grateful to our families for their patience and tremendous support throughout the writing of this book.

Mark S. Beasley
Frank A. Buckless

Chapter 1
The Light Goes On

"I wish this would last forever," kept running across Courtney's mind. This cruise had been a long time in coming, and at last she could relax. Sitting on the ship deck with her sister, she was beginning to unwind on their second day at sea. This trip was meant to be a celebration for getting her life back. The past three years had been a wild roller coaster ride with unimaginable business success. Now at 28, she was financially secure, with just over $1 million in the bank. It seemed like just yesterday she was beginning her career fresh out of college as a programmer for Interconnectivity Inc. Now she was in the money. But, there had been a significant personal sacrifice during the primetime of her life.

She could clearly remember sitting in her apartment one Friday night three years ago with her two closest work buddies, John and Brad, trying to decide what to do for fun. They were stressed from a wild and crazy week of cranking out source code – they just wanted some easy Friday night entertainment. They finally landed on Chinese food to be delivered, but were still in search of something to do. The thought of going to the movies was just too taxing. They finally settled on renting a movie, but no one had the energy to drive to the movie rental store. Then Brad commented, "Why don't they deliver movies like they do food?"

"Well, you still have to select the movie," observed Courtney. "It's hard to think of good movies without scanning the movie boxes on the shelves. I can never think of decent movies when it comes time for renting one without looking at what's current."

"You would think a local movie rental store would have a web site with movie selections and reviews," complained John. "Everything else is on-line now."

Brad jumped on John's comment, "Hey, wait a minute – we could do that!! We write Internet-based program code all day. We could design a cool search engine!"

"Yeah, right. When would we ever find the time?" whined Courtney.

* * * * *

Courtney, John, and Brad were in their third year of working at Interconnectivity Inc. They started together fresh out of college, as a part of the same programming training class for Interconnectivity, an Internet-based company located in Raleigh, North Carolina.

Courtney distinctly remembered how brash John was that first day. "Cocky, cocky, cocky" was all she thought after he came roaring into North Carolina as a hot-shot MIT electrical engineering graduate thinking he knew it all. He couldn't keep his mouth shut in their week-long orientation class, always having the last word to say. He was one of those high-energy types.

Brad, on the other hand, was as shy as they come. Intimidated by the room full of techies, he wondered whether he had made the right career choice. He wasn't sure why Interconnectivity hired him, given his degree in English from a small, west-coast liberal arts school. The recruiting process got him fired up, and the thought of heading to the east coast offered a great chance for change from his growing up days in California. He was intrigued by the opportunity to try something really different. He often wondered if all the recruiting hype had blinded him to the reality of his new programming job.

Courtney entered Interconnectivity having just graduated with honors from North Carolina State University, with a computer science degree. She came to NC State on one of the university's most prestigious scholarships. That provided her a full ride for tuition and books and numerous opportunities to engage in other educational experiences outside of her classes, including one summer abroad in Paris and a second summer camping with Outward Bound. Courtney was confident she was qualified for the job, and was excited to finally be on her own, earning a paycheck.

Brad and Courtney hit it off immediately, given their interest in reading fiction. She and Brad had challenging discussions of recent novels they were reading. Both found it amazing to see how they could have two different perspectives of the same novel. John never read fiction and kept changing the conversation to reviews of the latest technology toys. John and Brad became good friends, spending lots of time training for a marathon. Both were avid runners who liked to spend some of their Saturday mornings on long runs together.

Somehow, they all became inseparable. While John's exterior was obnoxious, Courtney and Brad soon realized that John was a loyal, giving friend. Over time they began to tease each other about their different personality traits and recognized the benefits of their differences.

They found their work at Interconnectivity challenging. The company, as a designer and host of Internet-based sites for small to medium-sized businesses, was quickly becoming a technology leader. Serving as a web site design outsourcer for clients, Interconnectivity had developed a niche providing technology support to clients wanting a sophisticated web presence.

Courtney, Brad, and John worked in the software programming group, largely responsible for creating source code used to support client web sites. The early days of the e-commerce boom were a huge success for Interconnectivity as it tapped into an incredible market and growth opportunity. Like many other technology companies, Interconnectivity was suffering from the recent downturn in the economy. As a result, Interconnectivity was expanding its services into other technology markets to compliment the e-commerce consulting it provided. Several new projects related to information systems assessments and enterprise-wide software installations for new clients were in process.

While they rarely worked on projects together, Courtney, Brad, and John frequently shared programming tips. John was particularly creative in his techno tricks, and generously shared source code ideas with the other two. All three were performing exceptionally well at Interconnectivity and were regularly assigned to very involved, complex projects.

While gaining tremendous programming experience, all three were feeling the pressure of adjusting to the demands of the professional life. They had less and less down time, often taking work home in order to get everything done. It was one of those things they could never let go of, often worrying about work demands in their off hours. Their frequent Friday night brain dumps gave them a chance to unwind and reinvigorate for the next week's work.

They believed their work pace would likely continue for years, having observed the grueling demand placed on those who worked above them. All three longed for more control over their day-to-day activities. Occasionally they dreamed of leaving their jobs to live in a more carefree manner. John often talked of joining the Peace Corps, while Courtney longed for her student life again. Brad just wanted to camp out at his parent's beach house for a year or two to write his novel.

With all this flashing through Courtney's mind that Friday night in her apartment, she thought John had totally lost his mind when she realized that he was really serious about investigating this movie rental business. How could they ever find time to create a web-based movie search engine, given their demanding work schedules?

What surprised her most was when Brad chimed in that Friday night saying, "I'd rather be writing source code for my own project than writing source code for my clients. We could really do this. Think about it, if we hit it big with this, we could have the control we long for. I could finally live at the beach working on my novel and you two could go off to the Peace Corps and to school. There must be tons of people exhausted like us on Friday nights who would like on-line movie selection with home delivery. All we would have to do is write a simple web-based index of available movies and hire a bunch of college students to deliver them. We could do it like my dry cleaners, which has a weekly delivery schedule where they pick up my clothes each Monday and return them each Thursday. We could do the same thing – deliver the movies on Thursdays and Fridays and pick them up on Tuesdays and Wednesdays."

* * * * *

Over the next several weeks, Courtney grew sick of Brad and John's continual brainstorming of the idea. But one day while waiting to have her hair cut, she picked up a recent issue of *Rolling Stones* magazine and saw an article about digitally downloading music via the Internet. Then the light clicked on in her mind. Maybe John and Brad were on to something. If they could create customer loyalty for a simple web-based movie selection site, they might be in a position to capitalize on their customer base if digital movies become readily available for easy Internet download. Their web presence could line them up perfectly to be one of the first to offer digital movie downloads, once that kind of technology is readily available for easy use. Furthermore, their business would still have the traditional "brick and mortar" presence given that they would still have a store where customers could stroll the aisles looking for movies. The web-based movie selection and ordering system would build loyalty with customers who like to shop via the Internet. Offering both a traditional business approach and a business-to-consumer web interface would be important as the e-commerce marketplace was in a state of transition.

Brad was shocked when Courtney called from her car on the way back to the office suggesting they get together for dinner to further discuss the idea. After hanging up, Brad walked over to John's cubicle and said, "You won't believe what just happened. 'Miss Rain on Our Parade' just called wanting us to get together to brainstorm our movie web site idea. She thinks the web site might put us in a position to capitalize on the market whenever movies can be easily downloaded digitally."

That night at dinner, they decided to go for it. John and Courtney agreed to work together after hours writing source code for the movie index. They lived close to each other, making it easy to work together. Brad agreed to research the movie rental industry in order to get a sense for the costs of movies and other roadblocks that would complicate their jump into the movie rental market.

* * * * *

How funny it seemed to Courtney to be working so closely with John! She realized her first impressions of him had come full circle. At first, he seemed such an ego maniac, but now she was looking forward to meeting him every night. She found his high-energy approach to life exciting. His constant good mood and positive outlook were beginning to rub off on her. They agreed to meet at Courtney's apartment so she wouldn't have to drive home late at night.

Courtney soon found that during most days at work her mind was focused on creating the web site. She was amazed how much energy she and John had to work on the project each night, given their daily work demands. She was finding the creative brainstorming sessions with John enjoyable. And, they were making good progress on the movie index.

John on the other hand had been intrigued with Courtney from day one, and was excited to now have an excuse to spend time with her. She was smart, articulate, and thoughtful. He was beginning to care less about whether the business idea worked and more about just enjoying his one-on-one time with Courtney. John couldn't keep his mind off the nightly work sessions, although he thought more about how he looked each night, than thinking about source code.

While doing everything he could to catch her eye, John was frustrated by Courtney's lack of interest in him beyond the friendship level. He regularly cooked dinner for their sessions and was working out more to keep his body in shape. How ironic it was that Courtney seemed to have her energies focused squarely on the project, while John was allowing himself to be more distracted.

The most frustrating thing for John was Courtney's constant reference to Steve, her college flame. She met Steve in one of her science classes, their sophomore year. They were inseparable for the rest of their college days. Given they were both computer science majors, they made out their course schedules together and spent significant time studying and hanging out on campus with each other. Steve was a real movie buff, constantly keeping her up to date on the latest films. He was a walking Hollywood archive.

Romance between Steve and Courtney kicked in big time with thoughts of eventually getting married. But, it began to unravel when Steve's job in the Silicon Valley came through. It was too good of an opportunity for Steve to turn down, just like Courtney's offer from Interconnectivity. Both agreed that they could make the long distance relationship work, given email, cell phones, and airplanes. After taking a couple of years to professionally develop, they thought they would have ample opportunity to relocate to be closer to each other. While being apart was one of the hardest things they had ever done, they were committed to making it work.

Now with college over two years behind them, Courtney was beginning to wonder if she and Steve could make it work. She was pushing the idea of Steve relocating back to North Carolina. With his movie interest and his technical programming expertise, she knew he would be a perfect fit for their movie based web venture. However, no matter what she said, Steve didn't seem convinced that the movie rental idea was good enough to warrant his move back east.

Courtney began pushing for John to give Steve a call to see if he could convince Steve on the merits of the venture. This was the last thing John wanted, but Courtney was clueless. After several nights of discussing the call with Courtney, John finally decided to take the higher road and give Steve a call. As a friend, he realized that this might make Courtney happy.

Unfortunately when he phoned Steve to convince him on the merits of the movie rental venture, he quickly realized the movie rental venture wasn't the issue. Steve was incredibly enthusiastic about the web-based movie index. It was noticeably obvious that his new love life was keeping him in California. Steve just couldn't get up his nerve to tell Courtney.

Now John was in a real bind. How could Courtney be told about Steve – John sure didn't want to be the one to break the news. John convinced Brad that the two of them together should let Courtney know of Steve's latest developments.

* * * * *

When they did, Courtney took it hard. However, after a couple weeks of tears, she gradually focused more on the new movie venture and less on Steve. Courtney was becoming the energy behind the project.

Over the next several weeks, she realized the project was a great diversion from thinking about Steve. She poured even more time into developing the web site prototype of the movie selection index. Before long, they were close to having an initial product for Brad's review.

Brad had also made good progress in learning about the movie rental industry. He made contact with video and DVD wholesalers and got lots of information on costs, delivery times, and life expectancy of movies. He regularly visited movie rental stores in the area, taking notes on the number of movies in stock, the quantities of each film, the organization of movies, rental prices, and the presentation of movie information in each store.

He explored the Internet, looking at all types of available web-based industry information. He was pleased to learn that none of the local stores had any web presence, except the one national movie rental chain that provided location information for each store. Fortunately, that site offered no movie selection information. The more Brad learned about the industry, the more convinced he became about the potential for this project.

Discussion Questions

1.   What kind of information would you want to obtain to determine the feasibility of this business idea?

2.   Why would it be important for Brad, Courtney, and John to track the time they are currently spending on the development of the web-based index and the fact-finding search on the movie rental industry? How should they track their time?

3.   Should the time they are currently spending on the development of the idea eventually be reported as an asset (i.e., as a resource for the business) on their *MoviesDoorToDoor.com*'s financial statements? Why or why not?

4.   What are the advantages and disadvantages if the three friends own their own business versus work for Interconnectivity Inc.?

5.   What strains can be placed on your personal and family life when starting your own business?

6.   What types of individuals would you approach for advice about starting your own business?

7.   Describe Brad, Courtney, and John's business planning process. How did they investigate the feasibility of their venture? What might they have done differently?

8.   What are the perils of mixing romantic with business relationships?

Chapter 2
Begging the Parents

The three months that followed their initial brainstorming session had really flown. Brad was pumped on Friday night as he anticipated the weekend meeting during which they planned to test the prototype web site index and pour over his industry information. Thoughts like, "We're going to hit a home run with this venture!" often ran through his mind. A good night's sleep would be critical, particularly since he wanted to get in a long run Saturday morning as part of his marathon training. But, he just couldn't unwind. After tossing in bed, he finally fell asleep on the sofa in front of the television about 2:00 a.m.

If it hadn't been for the Saturday cartoons blaring from the television, he might have slept past noon. Realizing it was after 8:00 am, he jumped up, threw on his running shoes and settled for a short three-mile run. Frustrated that he couldn't keep his planned 13 mile run and still be on time to Courtney's apartment for the weekend meeting, he focused on running especially hard to release some steam.

Grabbing a breakfast bar as he stepped out of the shower, he threw on jeans and a t-shirt and ran out the door to his car about 9:00 am, knowing he was going to be 15 minutes late. He thought about calling Courtney, but concluded he was better off just getting there. He hoped John would live up to his normal reputation of always being 15 to 20 minutes late.

To his surprise, John was already working with the computer demo when Brad walked into Courtney's apartment at 9:15. Courtney was making coffee and offered some bagels. Brad, still hungry as he tried to wind down from his crazy morning's start, grabbed a bagel and settled down with his coffee.

"John, let me see the computer screen," noted Brad. "Wow, that's awesome!" Brad couldn't believe the opening screen could be so flashy. "Let me have a closer look." Quickly, Brad's morning frustrations were erased.

"Wait a minute," replied John. "Let's get Courtney over here before we run through the web site. Courtney, come on! Brad is anxious to see this thing."

Courtney and John started walking Brad through the web index prototype. The opening page had great color, and the graphic animation was cool. The continual scrolling of the company name "*MoviesDoorToDoor.com*" looked just like the introduction of a movie and the side bar selections of movie categories looked just like a state of the art theatre marquee.

John started clicking on each of the movie categories in the side bar. The first category, "New Releases," started with a movie clip of an upcoming release. Brad was amazed that Courtney and John had been able to get hold of it. Following the clip, the site highlighted new movie releases by category-- Comedy, Suspense, Romance, Action, Classics, Children's, and Documentary.

"Let me see what you did for the other categories," Brad requested.

Courtney then showed Brad the other side bar links, which organized older releases by movie category. She showed how each category started with a short clip from a movie from that category. Brad couldn't believe that a different movie clip randomly appeared each time a category was selected. With the side-bar listing of categories always visible, Brad thought the web site was very user-friendly. He was amazed at the extent of information Courtney and John had already compiled for each movie listing.

John and Courtney then explained how customers would select a movie. Brad laughed when they entered his telephone number as the customer. They already had him in the database. "You really missed your calling as salespersons," Brad commented. "I'm sure you guys have already entered every family member and friend you know into our customer database. You obviously don't want to miss any rental opportunities."

Courtney laughed, "Yeah, but will they pay us?"

John then showed Brad how customers would register and place movie orders and confirm delivery times and addresses. After reviewing other features in the system, Brad said, "It looks like you guys have thought of everything. Could you show me how a customer will know when we will pick up a movie after they have viewed it?"

After a short pause, Courtney responded, "Oh, man. I can't believe we forgot to indicate the pickup date. That's something that John and I will have to add."

John threw his hands up in frustration. "I hate to go back into the source code again!" he moaned.

"Come on, John, don't get too down on yourself," responded Brad. "This web site is unbelievable. You and Courtney have really done it right. I'm amazed at the detail that is already incorporated. If all we have to do is deal with the movie return issue, we're still in great shape."

Brad sat back in utter shock and began to realize the amount of time Courtney and John had spent on developing the prototype. He was beginning to feel uneasy about the extent of his contribution relative to theirs. He hoped that the information he was going to share would be valued as much by Courtney and John. He was unsure whether they would perceive his effort as providing his fair share to the project. Obviously, Courtney was using this project as a nice diversion from thinking about Steve.

"I need a bathroom break," chimed John.

Courtney replied, "Oh my gosh. It's already 2:00 o'clock! I'm starving. Brad, can't we cover some of your information over lunch?"

"Sure, I can take my laptop with us."

* * * * *

They were quickly seated once they got to the restaurant. After being at their table for a while, they started wondering if a waitress had been assigned to their table. John finally flagged down a waitress who could take their order.

Once the waitress left with their order, John said, "Man, she's cute and seems to have a great personality. Hey, Brad you should ask her out!" After a moment's pause, John teased Brad again by saying, "I take that back. A woman that nice wouldn't go out with a geek like you!"

"John, I wonder about you. You can be so insensitive at times," responded Courtney. "Men, you're all alike - totally insensitive! Your animal-like instincts just amaze me."

"Courtney, lighten up," said John defensively. "I was just teasing the guy. Brad needs to be more aggressive at chasing women. I'm just trying to push him a bit."

"Come on, John," responded Courtney. "Look at Brad. You're making him turn red."

"Enough of this stuff," noted Brad. "We're never going to get out of here if we don't get back to business."

At that moment, the waitress came back with their drinks. Brad couldn't help from turning red, especially when John gave him a wink. All of a sudden, the waitress accidentally dropped a glass of water on Brad. He jumped out of his seat immediately, when the ice water hit him. The waitress was so embarrassed that she turned red. She kept apologizing as she grabbed napkins to wipe the water off of him. John started to laugh. He couldn't have set this up any better. Even Courtney was beginning to lose it. The waitress, of course, was oblivious to the prior conversation, and was puzzled as to why John and Courtney found this so humorous.

Sensing that the waitress was becoming more uncomfortable, Courtney began to apologize, "The three of us have been a little uptight lately. This is a great ice breaker."

"What a pun, Courtney," chimed John.

All four of them laughed. The waitress then said, "I guess I've lost my tip for today."

"Actually, I think you've just increased it," said John. "My name is John. My friends are Courtney and Brad."

After the waitress introduced herself, John then said, "Are you dating anyone currently? My friend here is available."

The waitress turned bright red. "He looks like a great guy, but I do have a boyfriend."

"Please try to ignore John," Brad said to the waitress. "He tries to embarrass me every chance he gets."

Once the waitress left, Courtney said, "John. Where did you learn your social skills? You're making a fool out of all of us!"

"Hey, she's okay with it," said John. "You don't get anywhere in life if you don't ask. I was just trying to help Brad out."

Brad responded, "I don't need help. I can handle things myself. We need to get back to why we came here. Let me tell you about the information I've obtained on the movie rental industry."

Brad began to provide information he researched about the movie rental industry. "Boy, both traditional VHS-formatted videos and DVD movie versions are much more expensive than I realized. I thought the cost would be in the $15-$20 range for any movie we might want. I was shocked to discover that purchases of new movies to be rented commercially are significantly more expensive than old releases. Most new movie releases range between $70 and $80 a piece, which is significantly higher than the $20-$30 price range for older releases and children's movies."

"Wow! How many movies do you think we'll need to buy?" asked Courtney. "This could quickly add up to a big price tag."

"What?! I don't have tons of money to sink into this," said John. He felt like the air was quickly coming out of their balloon.

Then Brad jumped in and said, "Wait a minute. It's not over yet. Let's not panic. Let me go through more details before I get to the money issue."

Brad began to describe how he thought they should build their movie library. From all his movie rental store visits, he estimated that they would need a beginning core of 250 older movie titles on the shelf to effectively compete with local movie rental stores. At this point he was targeting only one copy of each movie title just to get them going. He estimated a total up-front expenditure around $6,500 for the older movie releases.

250 movies X $25 average price per movie = $6,250

He went on to describe that for new releases they would need to start with 20 recent movie titles, with anywhere from two to 20 copies of each new release in a mix of VHS and DVD formats. "Let's assume we buy an average of 5 copies of 20 new movie releases to start, with each movie costing an average of $75. We'll spend about $7,500 just to stock up on new releases.

5 copies X 20 movie releases X $75 a piece = $7,500

Then, I anticipate that we will need to build our movie inventory by bringing in about five copies of two new titles a week at a cost of about $750 a week.

5 copies X 2 new movie releases X $75 a piece = $750

All this will depend on how popular certain releases are forecasted to be. I'll have to admit that anticipating a particular movie's popularity seems to involve a lot of guesswork."

"Now slow down," said John. "So what you're telling us is that we need $14,000 up front just to open the door with movies on the shelves." He wrote this on a scrap sheet of paper:

250 older release movies	*$6,500*
100 new movie releases	*$7,500*
Total Initial Movie Purchase Price	*$14,000*

John went on to say, "And, then we will be spending $39,000 in our first year just adding new releases to the library, if we spend $750 each of the 52 weeks in the year."

$$\$750 \times 52 \; weeks = \$39,000$$

Then John asked, "Is there any kind of tax break on all of this?"

"I don't know. I haven't even thought about the tax side of things," answered Brad.

"Well, I don't know about you, but I sure pay a ton of money in taxes each year and I assume that our business will, too, if we make money. We've got to factor taxes into every decision. Don't tax rates range anywhere from 10 to 40 percent of income?" asked John.

"I'll have to check into that," answered Brad. "You guys know I'm not an accountant."

Changing the subject back to the movie library, Courtney asked, "Do we have to keep all the copies of new releases forever?"

"No," answered Brad. "Once rentals of selected titles start to slow down, we can sell the extra copies to our customers for about $20 a piece."

"Just $20. Wow, we'll be losing tons of money if we buy new releases for $70 to $80 a piece. How will we ever make money this way?" asked John.

"John, don't forget that our main line of business is movie rentals," reminded Brad. "Hopefully, there will be repeated rentals of a single movie copy before we retire it for re-sale. We'll need to cover our movie purchase costs through our rental fees. So, when we get to the point of pricing our rental rates, we'll need to think this through carefully. And, don't forget, the movie will just be one of our costs in running this business."

Brad went on to describe the types of furniture and fixtures, computer equipment, store lease prepayments, phone and electrical hookup costs that would be needed to get the store up and running.

Brad noticed that Courtney was pushing food around her plate with her fork seemingly uninterested in hearing anymore.

John said, "What's up with you, Courtney?"

"These numbers are making me lose my appetite," moaned Courtney.

"Wait a minute," noted Brad. "Quit worrying about that. I've got an idea of how we can finance this startup."

"Okay, let's hear it," commented John.

"I mentioned this idea a couple of times to my dad," explained Brad. "You guys know that he started and runs his own company. Surprisingly, he is pretty excited about this idea – believe me, he doesn't get excited about much. But, he thinks this is something we should really pursue. He even hinted that he might be willing to front us some cash to help us get this business off the ground. Because he opened that door, I've been thinking that I should see how much he might be willing to cough up."

Courtney responded wishfully, "Does he have enough to cover everything we need to buy?"

"No way!" said Brad. "We're talking about a lot of money and I don't think he'll want to be the only person out on a limb."

"I mentioned this to my mom, too," offered John. "She seems to be very supportive of the idea. She's a physician, so she doesn't really understand market demand in the movie rental industry. But, she thinks the Internet market edge is intriguing, since she uses the Internet to research patient illnesses and to submit prescriptions to online pharmacies all the time. And, she expects that the use of the Internet to manage patient care is going to expand. She has never indicated whether she would be willing to provide any cash - I'm not sure how much she has. But being a single mom, she has learned to be savvy with her personal finances and investments. The good news is, she has always encouraged me to take risks. I'd be willing to ask her for some help."

Brad and John turned to look at Courtney to get her thoughts. Feeling a little awkward, Courtney finally responded. "Well, I've mentioned before that I don't have the greatest relationship with my parents. Not that we fight or anything, but we're not super close. My parents did give my brother and sister loans for their college education while my scholarships covered all my educational costs. Maybe they would be willing to give me some money to start this business since they didn't have to lend me money for college."

"Well, that's a workable idea," commented Brad. "Why don't we think about it a little more and try to see if our parents have any interest?"

John said, "This has been a productive day. It feels good to see how much great work has been done."

"Boy, you sure don't lack any confidence," Courtney said to John.

"When you've got it, you've got it," responded John. After a moment, he then asked Brad jokingly, "Hey, do you want to try to talk with the waitress one more time before we leave?"

"No. I think we've embarrassed her enough," said Brad. "Let's get out of here."

As they left, John walked by the waitress. As they passed each other, John teased her saying, "You'll let us know if you break up with your boyfriend?"

The waitress turned bright red again. Brad quickly said to her, "You don't need to answer that."

The waitress gave Brad a smile and said, "I won't. Thank you."

As they walked on, Courtney asked, "John, when will you ever learn that enough is enough?"

"Did you see that smile on the waitress' face?" asked John. "I think Brad has a chance!"

"Come on. I've had enough," responded Brad. "I'm going home."

* * * * *

Over the next couple of weeks, Brad had several long and grueling conversations with his dad concerning the viability of this business. His dad's experience in running his own company gave him the basis to ask questions that Brad and his cohorts hadn't even considered. Brad had a good handle on the actual expenditures to get the movies, furniture and computer in place, but had ignored the realities of all the operating expenditures that they would incur in the first several months of business.

Brad's dad forced them to project out what they thought might be a realistic expectation of their cash flows. He asked them to estimate the amount of cash coming in the door from customers and cash going out the door for buying more movies, paying the light bill, covering the building lease payments, fueling the car with gas for deliveries, and placing ads in local newspapers.

The threesome worked many nights trying to come up with a cash flow analysis for each of the first twelve months of the business. They struggled with it, given that they had to guess at the number of customers and rentals they would attract each month and at the costs that would vary depending on delivery volume.

First, they worked at estimating monthly cash outflows given that some of those numbers were easier to estimate. They already knew that it would take about $750 a week to buy new releases. So, they estimated the average monthly cost for new movie releases to be about $3,250 per month.

(52 weeks a year X $750 per week) / 12 months = $3,250 cost per month to purchase new movie releases

The building lease and other more constant monthly costs such as telephone, electricity, Internet Service Provider (ISP), and advertising costs added an additional $3,000 in monthly cash outlays. Estimating the gasoline costs was more difficult, given those costs would be dependent on customer volume and delivery location, which were less predictable. So, they decided to estimate customer rental volume next before guessing at gasoline costs.

They began to realize that the average monthly cash demand was approaching $6,500.

$3,250 for new movies + $3,000 for monthly operating expenses = $6,250

At that point, they tried to determine how many customers would have to rent movies for the business to be able to cover its costs. They checked out movie rental prices currently charged by local movie rental stores to get a feel for the price they could charge. They found that the local market charged $3.25 per movie on average. Given that part of *MoviesDoorToDoor.com's* market edge included home delivery, the threesome felt like the convenience to customers would allow them to charge an additional $.75 price premium. So, they initially decided to start with a rental price of $4.00 per movie.

But after some thought, they realized that their costs to deliver one movie versus delivering multiple movies to the same customer were the same. So, they modified their price structure to encourage multiple rentals at a time. They agreed on $4.00 for the first movie rented, and then $3.00 for each additional movie rented for that delivery. Based on their research, they estimated that customers would rent an average of 2.5 movies per order. They figured that this translated to an average rental price of $3.40 per movie as follows:

$$1^{st}\ movie\ X\ \$4.00\ each \quad = \$4.00$$
$$1.5\ movies\ X\ \$3.00\ each \quad = \underline{\$4.50}$$
$$Transaction\ Total \quad \underline{\$8.50}$$

Transaction Total of $8.50 / 2.5 movies rented = $3.40 average price per movie

Once they landed on a average rental price, they tried to estimate the volume of rentals they could generate in a month. Their game-plan was to open for business with 250 copies of older release movies plus 100 copies of new movie releases (5 copies of 20 new releases). That would give them 350 movie copies for rental on opening day.

With their plans to deliver movies on Thursdays and Fridays for subsequent pickup on Tuesdays and Wednesdays, they figured that each copy would be out on rental for 5 days. That meant they could rent the same movie on average 6 times a month. With the number of movies they would have in stock, they could rent a maximum of 2,100 movies in a month.

30 days in a month / 5 days out = 6 possible rentals a month
350 movies in stock X 6 rentals per month = 2,100 total rentals per month

While they knew it was unrealistic to assume that every movie copy would be rented 6 times a month, they decided to see how much cash they would generate under that assumption.

They really panicked when they realized that renting 2,100 movies a month for an average price of $3.40 would only generate $7,140 a month.

2,100 movies X $3.40 per movie = $7,140

That would barely cover their cash outflow needs, which were approaching $6,500. And, they noted that they hadn't considered any payroll costs and any return on the investment to owners. They had to go back to the drawing board.

They finally determined that they would have to change their business plan to have delivery and pickup occur nightly. Rather than only pickup movies on Tuesdays and Wednesdays, they decided that they would change their plans and pick up movies 2 days after rental. They would try to structure the pickups in certain locations as they delivered movies to other customers in those locations each night. By changing their pickup policy so that a movie would only be out for 2 days, they could increase the number of rentals each month. Using a best case scenario, they could rent a movie 15 times per month.

30 days / 2 days out on rental = 15 rental times per month

So, with their stock of 350 movies they could rent up to 5,250 movies per month.

350 movies X 15 rentals per month = 5,250 total movie rentals per month

That initially made them feel much better, given that using this best case scenario, they could generate $17,850 per month in rental fees.

350 movies X 15 rentals a month X $3.40 average price per movie =
$17,850 in cash for rental fees

Of course, they knew that kind of rental volume was totally unrealistic, particularly for the first few months of the business. They knew that renting all 350 movies for the maximum number of times in a month would never happen. So, to be much more conservative, they assumed that all movies couldn't be rented that much in a month. They broke down their estimate of likely rentals as follows:

1. They agreed that the 100 copies of new releases would likely be the most popular for renting. While under their new strategy a movie could be rented as much as 15 times a month, they estimated that the 100 copies of new movie releases would be rented 9 times a month on average. That would generate $3,060 per month.

100 new release copies X 9 rentals per month
X $3.40 average price = $3,060

2. They also figured that the 250 copies of older movies would be rented less frequently. Again, while they knew movies could be rented as many as 15 times per month, they decided that renting the 250 older movie releases 5 times a month would be feasible. That would generate an additional $4,250 per month.

250 old release copies X 5 rentals per month
X $3.40 average price = $4,250

Using these new figures, they estimated that the monthly rentals would generate $7,310 per month as follows:

Cash from rentals of new movie releases	*$3,060*
Cash from rentals of older movie releases	*$4,250*
Total Cash from Rentals per Month	*$7,310*

These more realistic estimates made them feel better. They knew there would be other costs they hadn't estimated. For example, there would be expenses related to employees, taxes, movie repair and replacement, and gasoline needed to deliver the movies, just to name a few. As a result, they knew they shouldn't expect much excess cash over their costs in the first year. It would take a while to build a loyal customer base. They agreed that looking beyond the first year would be necessary to see signs of stronger cash flows.

After pouring over these details a bit more, they realized that the estimated movie stock of 350 movies was conservative, too. Because they planned to add five copies of two new movie releases a week, they would be adding 43 movies to their movie stock each month.

10 new copies added per week X 52 weeks a year
/ 12 months per year = 43.33 movies added per month

At the same time, they knew they would be "retiring" some of the more dated new releases as popularity surrounding the new releases dropped. They figured that they would be taking an average of 6 copies off the shelf per week, which would generate 26 per month for re-sale.

6 movies removed per week X 52 weeks in a year / 12 months per year =
26 movies for re-sale each month

So, the net gain in movie stock per month was estimated to be about 17 movies.

43 new releases – 26 releases pulled off the shelf for resale = net gain of 17
movies per month

It also dawned on them that by the end of the first year they would build to a movie stock level of 554 movies. They would begin with 350 movies on opening day and add 17 movies per month for 12 months so they would have 554 movies at the end of the year. That meant that their monthly estimates of cash coming in from rentals should increase each month over the first 12 months, given that the number of movies that could be rented in a month would be increasing.

So, they revised their monthly cash inflow estimates by forecasting volume specifically for each month. For the first month, they worked with a stock of 350 movies. Then for the second month they worked with a stock of 367 movies (350 plus a net of 17 new movie copies), and for the third month 384 movies, and so on. They figured that even if their estimates of the number of rentals of a single movie per month was too high, the amount of cash from rentals should increase as their movie stock increased.

Now that they had a better handle on the number of movies to be rented in a month, they had a better basis to try to estimate their gasoline cost, which would be totally dependent on their delivery and pickup volume. They figured that their delivery area encompassed a 20-mile radius. But, given that they found a strip mall store-front close to a heavy residential area, they believed that most of their business would be within 5 miles of their store. So, they began to work more on estimating their monthly gasoline costs.

Working with the previous assumptions, here's how the delivery trips would look. They would rent:

1. 100 new movies an average of 9 times per month = 900 movies rentals
   plus
2. 250 older movies an average of 5 times per month = 1,250 movie rentals

So, they would need to deliver 2,150 movies a month consisting of 900 new and 1,250 older movie rentals. If their assumption that the average customer rents 2.5 movies for each rental transaction was accurate, they concluded that the number of delivery trips they would have to make would be 860 deliveries each month.

2,150 movies to be delivered / 2.5 movies delivered per customer order =
860 trips

Once they estimated the likely number of trips they would have to make, they then tried to estimate the number of miles they would drive each month to make the deliveries. They decided to estimate that each delivery trip would be less than ten miles on a round-trip basis, given that their heaviest volume was expected to be within 5 miles of their store. That meant that they would be driving an estimated 8,600 miles per month to deliver 860 rentals an average of 10 miles per delivery.

860 deliveries X 10 miles per delivery = 8,600 miles driven per month

Then they remembered that they would be able to make multiple deliveries in one trip. So, they decided that they could make five rental drop-offs and pickup five previously rented sets of movies during each trip away from the store. They estimated that coordinating the drop-offs and pickups in nearby areas would increase the roundtrip mileage to 20 miles per trip. Since each delivery would involve the drop-off of five customer orders, they determined that they would need to make about 172 trips away from the store each month, with each trip averaging 20 miles.

860 delivery orders to be made / 5 orders delivered per trip =
172 trips per month

That meant they would be driving 3,440 miles per month.

172 trips X 20 miles per trip = 3,440 miles driven per month

With gas averaging $1.80 per gallon and their cars averaging 18 miles per gallon, they estimated their gasoline costs to be approximately $350.00:

3,440 miles divided by 18 miles per gallon = 191.11 gallons of gas required
191.11 gallons required X $1.80 a gallon = $344.00

Finally, to pull it all together, they wrote down all the estimates they had made:

Estimated cash inflow:		
Monthly rentals	$ 7,310	(2,150 rentals @$3.40 ea.)
Monthly movie sales	$ 520	(26 movies sold @$20 ea.)
Total Cash Inflows	$ 7,830	
Less estimated cash outflows:		
Buying movies	($ 3,250)	
Utilities, Lease & Other	($ 3,000)	
Gasoline	($ 350)	
Total Cash Outflows	($6,600)	
Net Cash Flow	$ 1,230 per month	

Assuming this was a reasonable estimate of net monthly cash inflows, they projected their net cash flow for the year to be $14,760.

$1,230 net cash flow per month X 12 months = $14,760

They were satisfied with this estimate, given the realization that they couldn't expect significant increases in cash during the first year of business.

If they stayed with their plan to purchase new movie releases each week, they would have 554 movies in stock by the end of the year. Thus, the number of movies available each month would be increasing throughout the year, which should lead to more cash from customer rentals. And, they also hoped that their customer base would be growing at the same time.

Out of curiosity, they decided to calculate their net cash inflows for the last month of the first year when 554 movies would be available for rental. Of that, they figured there should be about 100 copies of new movie releases and 454 copies of older releases. Working with their earlier assumptions, they figured that they would be generating $10,778 in movie rentals by the end of the last month of the first year, which they calculated as follows:

100 new releases X 9 rentals a month X $3.40 per rental = $3,060
454 older releases X 5 rentals a month X $3.40 per rental = $7,718
Total Cash Inflows in Month #12 $10,778

That meant they would be renting new releases 900 times a month and renting old releases 2,270 times a month. So, they would have a total of 3,170 rentals a month.

100 new releases X 9 rentals per month =		*900 rentals*
454 new releases X 5 rentals per month =		*2,270 rentals*
Number of Rentals in Month #12:		*3,170 rentals*

Assuming that their monthly expenses remained the same as they forecasted earlier, their estimated net cash flow for the last month of the first year should be about $4,538. Here's how they calculated that:

Estimated cash inflow:

Monthly rentals	*$10,778 (3,170 rentals @$3.40 ea.)*
Monthly movie sales	*$ 520 (26 movies sold @$20 ea.)*
Total cash inflows	*$11,298*

Less estimated cash outflows:

Buying movies	*($ 3,250)*
Utilities, Lease & Other	*($ 3,000)*
Gasoline	*($ 510)*
Total Cash Outflows	*($6,760)*

Net Cash Flow	*$ 4,538 per month*

Now they felt much better!! They estimated that they would generate about $34,000 of cash net of expenditures for their first year of operation.

Net cash flow in the 1st month	*$1,230*
Net cash flow in the 12th month	*$4,538*
Sum	*$5,768*
Average Monthly Net Cash Flow	*$2,884 ($5,768 / 2 = $2,884)*
X 12 months	*X 12*
Projected Net Cash Flows in Year 1	*$34,608*

While knowing the first year wouldn't generate huge returns to them personally, they felt like the long-term potential for significant cash increases was promising. The first few months would likely be the toughest, as they worked to build the customer base and movie inventory. Knowing they might experience a few months with more cash being used than generated by rentals, they hoped future months would soon help make up for earlier months of cash squeezes.

They agreed that they should all sleep on this information for a few days and then approach their parents with the idea of possibly providing some initial funding to get the business up and running.

Discussion Questions

1. How does a business account for purchases made for items that will be used for years, like the money spent for the movies, the shelving, and the computer?

2. Do you think this business is likely to be profitable? What costs have they failed to consider in their initial analysis?

3. What are the corporate federal income tax rates, and what other taxes must be paid by the company? Would the state and local sales taxes be deducted from the $3.40 per movie, or would sales taxes be over and above the $3.40 per movie?

4. How does one go about reserving a web site address on the Internet?

5. If they do get the money from their parents, what costs, if any, might be associated with the money received from people outside of Courtney, Brad, and John?

6. The business proposal is based on cash projections. They didn't include any types of non-cash expenses in their analysis. Should non-cash expenses be reflected in a business's financial statements? What are some of the non-cash expenses *MoviesDoorToDoor.com* will likely incur?

7. How might changing movie and audio technologies (e.g., DVD vs. VHS format) affect *MoviesDoorToDoor.com's* financial projections?

8. When they projected cash flows expected for the 12th month of the first year, they forecasted their gasoline costs to be $510 (when they would have 554 movies available for rent). Using the same assumptions they made to forecast gasoline costs in the first month of operations, show how they arrived at the $510 estimate.

Chapter 3
Starting the Business

The business proposal was finally written and ready to go to their parents, but Brad just couldn't get up his nerve to hit the email "send" button to zap it to his dad. He felt like the three of them had done a good job of thinking through the first year of operations. However, given his dad's business savvy and experience, he feared his dad would rip the proposal apart. While Brad and his dad had a great relationship, he knew that because money was involved his dad would be critical of the proposal.

Brad kept thinking how ridiculous it was for him to be so nervous about sending the email with the attached proposal. Finally on Monday he told himself to "just do it" and he quickly hit the send button. It was gone. In his email note accompanying the proposal, Brad asked his dad to read the proposal within the next couple of days, and that Brad indicated that he would call him on Thursday night to get his reaction.

Brad was shocked on Thursday when he answered the phone and his dad was on the line. While Brad was planning to call him that night, his dad beat him to the punch.

"Son, I just finished reading through the proposal and I'm impressed at how professional you guys have been in thinking through the various issues related to your proposed business idea. I guess that English degree in college is going to pay off after all! You guys did a great job writing the business plan."

Brad was pumped to hear his dad's enthusiasm about the business idea. Fifteen minutes into the telephone conversation, Brad found himself wondering what he had missed in the earlier parts of the conversation. Brad never thought his dad would react so positively. Of course his dad raised some good issues. For example, his dad was really questioning whether they could deliver that many movies in a night by only working 5:00 p.m. to 11:00 p.m. daily. His dad was also concerned about Interconnectivity's reaction to learning about this new company being created on the side and whether Interconnectivity could ever assert any legal rights to the web site. His dad was relieved to hear that all the development of the site was based on purchased software installed on their home computers. Brad made it clear that their development activities were done after hours and none involved the use of Interconnectivity resources. After hearing that, Brad's dad felt like Interconnectivity wouldn't have legal rights to their work on the web site.

"Brad, what worries me most is your ability to work two jobs, especially given the fact that much of your time will involve your driving all over town after a long day's work at Interconnectivity," noted his dad. "You won't have much personal life. And, I would hate for physical exhaustion to set in, putting you at risk. You need to make sure you stay focused on your main job. The last thing you need to do is to neglect your commitment to Interconnectivity by letting the quality of your work fall. Remember that a high percentage of new businesses fail. So, you need to think of your job at Interconnectivity as your life's main support for quite a while. Even though your business proposal indicates a positive cash flow each month, there won't be enough cash generated for the three of you to be able to support yourselves for quite a while, which assumes your business even survives. And, remember you are merely forecasting the future with no real certainty that you will be able to rent the number of movies you project. In fact, that's where you've probably been the most unrealistic. I doubt that you will be out of 'the red' for several months or even years, at best."

"What do you mean by out of 'the red'?" asked Brad.

"Well, when you are in 'the red' you have more cash going out than coming in. You obviously want to shoot for being in 'the black' which means you are generating more cash than you are spending," responded his dad.

Brad's dad then went on a diversion and began to tease him about his mom's reaction. "She is most concerned about how creating this new company would leave no time for you to socialize. You'll have a lot less time for a love life anyway. Maybe you could solve this dilemma by starting up a little something with Courtney."

"Oh, Dad, give me a break. Courtney and I are just good friends. Besides, John seems to be the one chasing her. And, remind Mom that I'm still young. I have plenty of time for that later," answered Brad.

That prompted his dad to express some concerns about how Brad would be able to protect his financial interests in the company if John and Courtney became an item.

Brad responded that Courtney seemed to have no interest in John. John, being his usual self, was more intrigued with the chase knowing he would probably not win her over. Brad noted that the three of them were really good friends. They had been working together at Interconnectivity and they spent most of their time off together. Brad was confident this wouldn't become an issue.

His dad quickly answered back, "When mixing money with friends or relatives, the dynamics of the relationship can change. I'm not saying you shouldn't do it, I just want you to go into this venture with your eyes wide open." He emphasized the importance of their legally formalizing all aspects of the business and warned Brad not to let the friendship blind him to the need to have everything in writing. He noted that at some point one of the three may want out of the business. They needed to think of hypothetical scenarios that could occur and identify now how they would react to those situations.

Then the big question came. "Where are you going to get the start-up cash?" asked his dad.

Brad took a deep breath and said, "Well, Dad......I was hoping you might be interested in fronting us a little cash."

The silence on the other end was deafening. Finally, his dad responded with "How much are you talking about?"

Brad started reviewing their cash needs as outlined in their proposal. He first pointed out the $14,000 needed to establish the movie library of 350 movies for opening day. Then he described other one-time cash outlays such as the building lease deposit, the purchase of store shelving units, computer equipment, minor store front renovations, advertising, and legal fees to formalize the business, which they estimated at about $20,000.

"So, Dad, we think we need about $34,000 to open our doors," summarized Brad.

"Whoa, I think you need a lot more than that. What happens if you don't have as many customers as you expect? Your proposal lays out about $6,600 in monthly cash outlays, which are mostly fixed expenses and not based on customer volume. How would you cover those costs in the event you rent fewer movies than you project? I would recommend that you create a cash reserve of $20,000 should your cash inflows not be as strong as you forecast. That would cover about three months of your expenses in the event you had no revenues. A reserve like that should help bridge you through the first year when your monthly net cash flows are likely to be quite low." His dad continued, "My guess is that it will take several years before you have a loyal enough customer base to provide a sufficient cash inflow."

"You mean you think we need $54,000 to open our doors? Man, that's a lot of money," answered Brad. "Dad, are you willing to help us? How much would you be able to chip in?"

"Son, I'll tell you what. If you can get your two partners to each come up with a third, I would be willing to cover the remaining third. I know the U.S. federal tax laws allow your mom and me to give you $20,000 together on an annual basis without triggering an estate tax problem. But, I will have to touch base with my tax accountant to make sure the funds can be distributed without creating a tax issue. To be fair to your brother and sister, this gift would be reduced from your share of our estate in the event of our death."

"Wow, Dad! You and Mom are being very generous. Thanks for your support and encouragement," noted Brad.

"We are very proud of you, son, and are glad we are in a position to help. And, we think you guys have a great business plan and want to do what we can to help you launch it. But remember, we expect your help in our retirement days when you hit it big! Don't forget us then!" responded his dad.

"Since Courtney, John, and I didn't anticipate this kind of cash need to start the business, I need to follow up with them to see if they think they can come up with the other two-thirds. You guys have really made it easy for me. I'll touch base in a few days." Brad and his dad caught up on the latest family happenings before saying goodbye.

Brad was so excited about his telephone conversation with his dad he immediately called John. When John answered the phone, Brad asked abruptly, "Do you want the good news or bad news first?"

"Tell me the good news first," responded John.

"Well, my dad is willing to front a third of our initial cash needs. The bad news is that he thinks it will take us at least $54,000, not $34,000, to get the business up and running."

"Why so much more than we anticipated?" questioned John.

"My dad is concerned that we haven't left ourselves enough cushion to cover any negative cash flows. He thinks our estimated customer rentals are overly optimistic for the first few months. He believes it will take us longer to develop a loyal and reliable customer base than we projected. He wants us to have a sufficient cushion to cover negative cash flows that could be incurred because of low rental volumes in the first year. Look at it this way, the extra $20,000 will cover our monthly projected cash outflows for three months assuming a worst-case scenario where we have no rentals.

$6,600 cash outflow per month X 3 months = $19,800

He convinced me that this is the best way to go."

"Okay, but I have already talked with my mom. She agreed to invest about $11,000 (about a third of the original $34,000 initial cash needs). I'm not sure she'll buy-in to increasing that. She made it clear to me that this would have to be viewed as another one of her investments and would not be a gift from her to me. So, she would expect a reasonable return on her investment. As you know, she is on her own and can't afford to just drop us a large sum of cash without having some strings attached."

"What does that mean?" questioned Brad. "What does she expect from us?"

"I guess she expects shares of stock and some periodic cash payments," answered John. "She is used to receiving regular dividend payments and interest income from her other investments. So, she would also expect our company to grow in order for her investment to appreciate in value over time. I think she will be reasonable in her investment return expectations, since this company does involve her son. But she will be looking for some mixture of stock appreciation and periodic cash payments."

"Since my dad and mom are giving me the money free and clear, does that mean my ownership interests will equal your mom's interest and you won't have any?" asked Brad.

"I hope not," answered John. "Surely I get a piece of the pie for all the work involved in creating and running this business. I keep hearing about executives who receive stock options from their companies. I just assumed we would each start out with having some ownership as compensation for all our time and effort in starting and running the business."

"I guess you're right," answered Brad. "We should assign equal shares of ownership among the three of us to cover our time and effort and then issue additional shares to those willing to provide financial resources."

"Wait a second. Does this mean I will have a smaller ownership interest than you?" asked John.

"How's that?" asked Brad.

"Well, you'll get shares for your work towards getting the business up and running plus the shares you'll buy with your parent's gift to you," noted John.

"Yeah, you're right," responded Brad. "But assuming your mom antes up the full one-third, then the combined interests for you and your mom will equal mine. Doesn't that seem fair? In reality this issue is between my parents and me and between you and your mom. We have to be fair to all parties contributing to this business."

After a pause, John said, "Okay, that seems reasonable. I can't think of a better arrangement. Brad, you better give Courtney a heads-up about the higher cash need. I hope she hasn't approached her parents yet. You know, her relationship with them isn't as good as ours with our parents. It might be hard for her to go back to them again to ask for more."

* * * * *

Brad was relieved when he called Courtney and learned that she hadn't talked with her parents about the business proposal. Brad explained to Courtney why the anticipated opening door cash needs had grown from $34,000 to $54,000. He went on to explain, "Courtney, my parents are going to give me the money as an early inheritance. That means I will actually use the money to invest in our company for myself. John's mother, on the other hand, has agreed to invest personally in our company. So, in that case, she will actually be a part owner of the business."

"Brad, I've already told you guys that the best I think my parents will do is loan us the money," explained Courtney. "I seriously doubt that they are interested in owning an interest in the business."

"Man, you and John are making this difficult," responded Brad.

"Hold on," responded Courtney defensively. "We're doing our best to get the funds we need. You can't blame us for having parents who are not in position to just give us money. I think we are fortunate that they are willing to help in the best way they can. There are a lot parents out there who would have no ability to do anything in situations like this."

"Well, John is telling me that his mom has to be a partial owner of the business and you're telling me that your parents don't want to be owners. So, I have no idea how we are supposed to handle this. We're going to need an accountant to explain all this to us," noted Brad.

"You know, I have a friend from college who majored in accounting and now works for one of the big international accounting firms. I'll give her a call to see what she says," offered Courtney.

"That would be great. When do you think you can touch base with your parents?" asked Brad.

"I usually talk to my parents on Sundays. So, I'll ask them then," responded Courtney.

* * * * *

With a sigh of relief, Courtney hung up the phone. Her conversation with her parents that Sunday went better than expected. She hadn't been certain they would be willing to lend the new business any money. However, they agreed to loan the company $18,000 with the understanding that they would receive an annual interest payment at an 8% interest rate. They also made it clear that the company would have to pay back the $18,000 at the end of five years.

Courtney was so excited with the good news that she immediately picked up the phone to call John. The phone rang continuously until finally after 15 rings John answered. "Hey John, it's me. What took you so long to answer?"

"Hold on, I'm on the other line," answered John. "Let me get off that call."

* * * * *

"Okay, I'm back," said John. "What's up?"

"Who was on the other line?" asked Courtney.

"Oh, it was Liza – an old friend who just moved from Boston to Raleigh," responded John.

"What kind of 'old friend'? Is this someone I should be concerned about?" asked Courtney. She couldn't believe how she was reacting. Immediately, a tinge of jealously kicked in. She never felt this way when she was dating Steve. However, the last several months of working with John on the web site had been so exciting and fun. She had begun to develop deep romantic feelings towards him. And then when John kissed her as he was leaving one night a couple of weeks ago, she knew the feelings must be mutual. She had high hopes about this new relationship. So, word of Liza was a little startling.

"Liza is someone I haven't seen in over three years," responded John. "She touched base with me a few times to get a sense for the lay of the land around here. Are you jealous?"

"No! Well, maybe a little. You know this thing between us is a little new and I haven't had feelings like this in a while. I just want to keep our relationship going," said Courtney.

"Come on Courtney, you have nothing to worry about. I feel too connected to you to jeopardize our relationship," responded John.

Courtney was relieved to hear John's reaction and said, "I guess I'm a little paranoid."

"Well, I'm in high demand these days," muttered John.

"What?" asked Courtney.

"Oh, nothing," quipped John.

After a little silence, Courtney said, "Enough of this mushy stuff. But, you know we really need to tell Brad what's happening with us. I really think he is clueless."

"I think you're right," responded John. "Brad did mention that his dad raised concerns about the potential of you and me starting a relationship. He told his dad it wasn't a big deal since you appeared to have no interest in me."

"Why is his dad worried about us?" asked Courtney.

"I think he's worried that our business relationship could become awkward if Brad or I entered into a romantic relationship with you. He thinks we ought to discuss what we would do if that were to occur," answered John.

"Okay, I can understand that," replied Courtney. "I must admit that I'm a little uncomfortable telling Brad about us."

"Let's think about that later," noted John.

"Hey, I never told you why I was calling," said Courtney. "I just got off the phone with my parents. They're going to lend us the money we need to start the business. They want us to pay them back the loan at the end of five years, along with annual interest payments."

"That's great. How do you think Brad will react to the loan idea?" asked John.

"I think we need more information," said Courtney. "I told Brad that I would talk to an accountant friend of mine to understand the differences between getting a loan and selling an ownership interest in the business. I'll call her tomorrow. Why don't you set up a time for all of us to discuss going forward with the business?"

"Sounds like a good plan" answered John.

* * * * *

Several days later, the threesome met for dinner to discuss Courtney's recent conversation with her accountant friend. Brad was surprised to find that he was the first to arrive at the restaurant for the meeting. He got a corner table for privacy.

His jaw dropped when John and Courtney approached the table hand-in-hand. He didn't know what to say. All he could think about was his conversation with his dad. He decided not to respond to what he saw.

John and Courtney were startled when they sat down at the table, given Brad's lack of reaction to their entry. Brad immediately inquired about Courtney's conversation with the accountant. Now they really felt awkward. They gave a few glances at each other, but decided to proceed with the conversation about the business issues.

Courtney responded, "I met with my friend, Rebecca, for lunch to discuss our situation. She was very helpful. Let me give you an overview of what she told me."

"Tell us!" said Brad.

Courtney explained, "Apparently, the different conditions placed by our parents on the uses of their money will trigger different legal obligations. Most start-up businesses have two primary methods to obtain outside financing for their businesses."

Courtney continued, "One method involves the issuance of stock and the relinquishment of some of the ownership in the business. The individuals who contribute resources (e.g., cash or other assets) to the business in exchange for stock and ownership are called stockholders. The business has no legal obligation to pay any funds to stockholders unless the business is liquidated or a majority of the stockholders vote to distribute some of the company resources. The most common way that resources are distributed to owners is in the form of cash, which is referred to as a "dividend." A significant consideration for us is the loss of control over all business decisions. Stockholders, as owners of the business, have voting rights that are in proportion to the level of stock ownership they hold. For example, if they own more than 50 percent of the outstanding shares, they can effectively control all business decisions."

"Okay. Now tell us about the other method," said John.

Courtney continued, "The other method involves borrowing funds from creditors like individuals, banks, insurance companies, and other financing institutions. In this situation, the business is normally legally obligated to repay the originally borrowed loan amount plus a financing charge. This financing charge is called interest. The good news is that this interest charge is deductible for tax purposes. Dividend distributions to owners, on the other hand, are not tax deductible for the business."

"Can they control the business decisions like stockholders?" asked John.

"A nice feature of obtaining funds from creditors is that they do not have any ownership interest in the business. Thus, they cannot directly influence day-to-day business decisions," responded Courtney. "Of course, the negative is that we have to make all loan and interest payments as stipulated in the agreement. Additionally, many of the loan agreements contain specific requirements that must be satisfied. These requirements are commonly referred to as debt covenants. An example of a typical debt covenant is that the lender may require the borrower to prepare and present audited financial statements annually. From what I understand, those audit costs are not small."

Brad jumped in, "Does this mean that John's mom will be a stockholder involved in making day-to-day business decisions, given she wants to be a direct investor in the business?"

"Well, she definitely will have the right to voice opinions about day-to-day business decisions. How much voice she has depends on the number of shares she owns compared to the number of shares we own," responded Courtney. "My parents, on the other hand, will not have a voice in the day-to-day operations of the business."

"How will the three of us get shares of ownership if we aren't contributing cash to the business?" asked John.

"Well, I'm going to pay cash," noted Brad.

"Yeah, I know that the money from your parents will allow you to invest cash in the business. But, as you know, neither Courtney nor I are in a position to contribute cash personally to the business. So, will we have any ownership interest?" inquired John.

Courtney piped in, "Based on my discussions with Rebecca, we should all receive a financial interest to reflect our non-cash contributions to this business. We've spent a lot of time and effort researching the business and designing our movie web site. For that contribution of labor, we should all receive shares of stock in our business. Rebecca suggested that we take the normal billing rate that Interconnectivity Inc. charges for web site development and multiply that by the total estimated hours we have invested in investigating, researching, and developing the business idea and related web site."

"Man, that's going to be a lot of money," chimed Brad.

"Well, it should be given all our efforts. We deserve to be fairly compensated for our hard work," answered John.

"Rebecca and I explored this further. I honestly think we have collectively contributed 500 hours to this project. If we use Interconnectivity's average billing rate of $100 per hour, the value of our contributions to the business at this point is $50,000. Thus, Rebecca recommended that we each be given credit for about $16,700 to the business," explained Courtney.

(500 hours x $100 per hour) / 3 people =
$$\$16,700 \text{ of value contributed per person}$$

Immediately, both Brad and John responded at the same time, "Sounds like a winner." Both began to laugh. John said, "Well, great minds think alike. Why don't we say that everyone's contribution to the start-up of the business was $18,000? That would equal the amount provided by our parents." They all agreed that was reasonable.

"Given the uncertainties of our business, Rebecca thought we should assign a low dollar value to each share of stock. She suggested that we assign a value of $5 for each share of stock we initially issue. So, for the $54,000 (3 X $18,000) sweat-equity contribution to the business by the three of us, we would each receive 3,600 shares of stock:

$54,000 / $5 per share = 10,800 shares
10,800 shares / 3 people = 3,600 shares per person

Brad will receive an additional 3,600 shares for the $18,000 contribution he will make using the proceeds from his parents ($18,000/$5 per share = 3,600 shares). John's mother will also receive 3,600 shares for her $18,000 commitment," noted Courtney.

"What about your parents, Courtney?" asked John.

"Well, remember, they won't be stockholders," responded Courtney. "So, they won't receive any shares of stock. But, we will have to sign a legal agreement stipulating that we will pay them 8 percent of the loan balance annually in the form of interest and repay the original loan amount at the end of five years."

"Let's make sure we all understand what the relative ownership rights will be," noted Brad. He sketched the following out on his napkin:

Ownership	Number of Shares	Percentage
Brad	7,200	40.0
John	3,600	20.0
Courtney	3,600	20.0
John's mom	3,600	20.0

Total	*18,000*	*100.00*

Brad started thinking back to his conversation with his dad. Given what he saw when John and Courtney approached the table, he began to understand the point his dad was trying to make. John, along with his mom and Courtney, would have a combined controlling interest of 60 percent of the business. Brad realized that effectively he would have no voice in the business, if all three decided to gang up on him. However, he recognized that they were collectively putting up more money than he was and if Courtney's parents had decided to take an ownership interest in the business, his ownership percentage would be even less. So, he realized that this was a risk he would have to be willing to live with if he wanted to go forward with this business. He also noted that for the additional risk he would be bearing, he would reap a greater percentage of profits than either John or Courtney.

They continued to discuss various implementation issues for the business. They all agreed that what they discussed sounded like a reasonable way to allocate the shares of stock in the business.

Brad couldn't hold on any longer. "What's the deal with you two?"

"We need to talk about it, but I've got to go. Let's talk tomorrow," responded Courtney as she stood to leave.

As Courtney took off, Brad and John decided to run together the next morning, since they usually met on Saturdays for a long run.

Discussion Questions

1. Brad's dad noted the importance of thinking about hypothetical scenarios that could occur in the future, and he encouraged them to formalize solutions to each scenario as they create the company. What are some of the future issues that should be formalized now?

2. How does an individual make money by purchasing stock in a company? What legal obligation does the company have for providing a reasonable return on the investment and for returning the proceeds from the original investment to investors?

3. The three founders are not taking any salary for at least the first year. Discuss whether it is reasonable for them to receive an ownership interest in the company for their time and effort. Describe your rationale to support your answer. Assuming that it is reasonable to provide the founders with an ownership interest for their time and effort, how would you determine how much that ownership interest should be relative to the ownership interest given to those investing cash in the business?

4.   Explain advantages and disadvantages of selling an ownership interest in the business versus borrowing money to finance operations.

5.   Briefly explain the differences between organizing a business as a sole proprietorship, partnership, or corporation. Explain why the sole proprietorship arrangement is not an option.

6.   Company financial statements include the Balance Sheet, Income Statement, Statement of Stockholders Equity, and Statement of Cash Flows. What financial statement would reflect the investments in the business by Brad and John's mother? What account title would be used to reflect those amounts?

7.   What financial statement would reflect the loan from Courtney's parents? What account title would be used to reflect that loan?

8.   How would the owner's equity account titles in the financial statements differ between a sole proprietorship, partnership, and corporation?

9.   Why would a creditor require a borrower to present audited financial statements on an annual basis?

Chapter 4
Buying Movies – Can't
Turn Back

Brad tossed all night wondering what was going on between John and Courtney. Would his dad's words come to haunt him? It looked to Brad like John and Courtney were now an item. What would happen if the relationship turned sour? Would they be able to continue working on a professional level? Would one of them want out of the business?

Brad began to realize that they needed to spell out the specifics of how they would handle a potential sell out of one of the original investors. He was concerned that the individual deciding to sell could sell to anyone, which could significantly change the dynamics of the business. Worse yet, no one may choose to sell out causing the business to fall apart due to their inability to work together to make business decisions. Brad was quickly realizing that they needed to come up with a plan that would spell out how they would establish a market value for each share of stock in the company, determine whether a sellout could be forced, and agree on some kind of buy-out plan for the remaining investors to be able to purchase the shares of stock over time.

"Wow, this is getting complicated," thought Brad. He never knew owning his own business could raise so many unforeseen issues. "What else haven't we considered?" wondered Brad. After what seemed like hours, he finally dozed off to sleep.

* * * * *

John met Brad the next morning at a local park where they usually went for long runs. They really enjoyed the scenic view on their 12-mile loop. It was hard to believe the park was in the center of urban sprawl, given the heavily wooded running trail.

"What's the deal with you and Courtney?" asked Brad soon after they met. He figured he might as well get the issue on the table at the beginning of the run to give them 12 miles to deal with it.

"We've been meaning to talk to you about this, but just didn't know how to present it to you," explained John. "For the longest time, we tried to keep things at a totally professional level. But, all those nights of working on the web site with Courtney helped me see all her great qualities. I quickly found that I really enjoy being with her. I realized how much I was attracted to her and could hold off no longer. Her ex-flame's decision to end their long-term relationship opened the door for Courtney and me. Once she was over Steve, she showed interest in me. That's when it all began."

"How do you know she's not on the rebound with you?" jabbed Brad. "Do you think your relationship will be long term?"

"You could be right about the rebound, but it sure doesn't feel that way to me," responded John.

"Well, if it is a relationship on the rebound, what does that mean for the three of us?" asked Brad. "Would we still be able to work together if it all dissolves? Don't forget we're going to be spending tons of hours each night manning the business. That might be tough if you two are no longer an item."

"Well, you're making some good points," responded John. "But, that may be water over the dam, since it's too late for us to turn back now. We're going to have to figure out a way to deal with that. I hope we are mature enough to handle whatever scenario arises."

"We need to spell out some of these issues now, so we can agree on how to address things like this if they arise," noted Brad. "We need to get an attorney who has experience with start-up companies to help us spell out details, such as a buyout plan."

"Yeah, you're right," noted John. "We also need an attorney to help us incorporate our business in North Carolina to limit our personal liabilities. Courtney noted last night that corporations have the benefit of limiting losses to the extent of the investment in the business whereas partnerships do not."

"Does that mean if our company is sued because one of our delivery people hits someone with a car, all that I can lose is my investment in the business and I won't have to worry about losing my car and other personal items?" asked Brad.

"I think so. But, we need to confirm all this with an attorney," answered John.

"I wonder why anyone would ever set their business up as a partnership?" asked Brad.

"I asked Courtney the same question. She indicated that the big negative of a corporation is that the business has to pay taxes on earnings, and investors have to pay taxes on the share of those earnings passed to them in the form of dividends. So, the same earnings are taxed twice, which is referred to as 'double taxation'. In contrast, a partnership only pays taxes on earnings once," described John.

"I can see that we do need an attorney," chimed Brad.

Brad was shocked when he realized that they only had a mile left in their run, which had gone by quickly given the intensity of their conversation. Later, as they were leaving the park, John and Brad agreed that each of them needed to identify an attorney.

* * * * *

As soon as John got to his apartment he picked up the phone to call Courtney. When she answered, John said, "The cat is out of the bag. Brad and I discussed our relationship. There are definite issues we need to resolve. But, in the end, he seems okay with it."

"What do you mean 'issues'?" asked Courtney. "Isn't this a personal matter between you and me?"

"Brad raised some good points like what happens if our relationship dissolves. We are going to be working together every night over the first year as we get the business up and running," answered John.

"I'm committed to this relationship. I don't think his concerns will be realized," responded Courtney.

"I'm committed, too," said John. "But, we need to have a clear arrangement on how we will deal with our breakup to provide some assurance to Brad that the business won't fall apart. This has helped me realize that we need to develop a buyout plan should any of us want out for any reason."

"I can understand that. Since we'll need an attorney to help us incorporate, we should have the attorney help us with this issue as well," noted Courtney. "I could check with Rebecca. I'm sure she has worked with some good attorneys on just these issues for her clients."

"That would be great. Can you touch base with her on Monday?" asked John.

* * * * *

Rebecca was right. The attorney she recommended, Garrett Hayley, was fabulous. He had great recommendations on how to incorporate the business and establish a buyout plan in the event one of the owners wants out. He was going to begin working on the "Articles of Incorporation" and the buyout provision agreement for their review in a week.

The next week was hectic. They received the $54,000 from their families, signed the legal documents, and wrote their first check out of the business to the attorney for his fees. While they hated to spend the first $3,000 on legal fees, Garrett's help was worth it.

It was exciting for Brad and Courtney to sign their first business check. When they opened the account, they decided that Brad and Courtney would be co-signers on all checks and John would be the record-keeper of all business transactions. They figured that was the best way to allocate responsibilities so that everyone would be aware of how money was being used.

"Let's go celebrate! We have $51,000 at our disposal. I feel like a wheeler-dealer, now," joked John.

"Great idea. Let's go to the Fox and Hound for dinner. They have a great English pub where we can celebrate before dinner," noted Courtney.

The celebration got a little out of hand with all the food and beverages they ordered. They were surprised when the dinner bill for $240 arrived. Fortunately, the restaurant would take a check. So, Brad and Courtney signed their second business check. They handed the receipt over to John for him to record in the check register.

* * * * *

Over the next several weeks, they spent a lot of money. They signed the building lease for the storefront, which required not only the first month's rent but also a significant deposit. They ordered movies, purchased shelving, hooked up store electricity, water, Internet access, and telephone. Courtney worked with a local advertising agency on some basic advertising brochures and flyers to help publicize the business. The advertising agency also helped them design a neat customer identification card that would be issued to all customers. They also purchased numerous business supplies, such as stationery, envelopes, among other things.

To save money, Brad, Courtney, and John decided to paint and install the shelving themselves. John's mechanical skills came in handy as they attempted to assemble the shelving. They were having a fun time working together at night. There were lots of jokes, laughs, and pizza, which made it hard to go back to Interconnectivity during the days for their cash-paying jobs. The movie store was really coming together.

The activity in the store caught the attention of several people walking through the shopping center. The threesome had several opportunities to describe the concept surrounding their new business. Most people reacted positively, which only increased Brad, Courtney, and John's enthusiasm. All this excitement made it difficult for them to do much else, including sleep. No one could remember going through something this exciting for such an extended period of time. They felt as if they were living on top of the world.

They also spent time getting the newly purchased computer system wired and installing the final version of the web site. It was neat for them to see the fancy new computer system in operation. There were three terminals located throughout the store that customers could use to search for movie ideas, in addition to the two terminals at the cashier section at the front of the store. The server was located in the back room of the store, in a storage closet away from day-to-day customer traffic. They were amazed at its speed and functionality. Courtney and Brad were really impressed at the great job John did in setting up the system. He definitely was not lacking confidence in his abilities, which annoyed the others occasionally.

To their surprise, the web-site was beginning to receive some attention from local people asking when they would be open. Apparently, registering the *MoviesDoorToDoor.com* web site with various search engines was already paying off. That only motivated the three to work even harder.

Soon after the store set-up was complete, the movies they had ordered began to arrive. The reality of having a real business was beginning to set in. When Brad opened the shipment of the first set of movies, he commented, "Well, I guess we can't turn back now."

Brad organized the display of the movies as they arrived. Courtney entered the actual movies received into their web-site database. She focused on entering information about all the various dimensions of the movies that customers might use to select movies off the web site. John focused on record-keeping.

Throughout all this craziness, John was using a shoebox to hold all the receipts from the business purchases made by Brad and Courtney. All the other activities made it almost impossible for him to start any formal system of record-keeping. When he finally settled down to record items, he couldn't believe how many receipts had accumulated in the shoebox. His first thought was, "Why did I let this build up to this extent? This could take days or weeks to organize." When he looked at the first receipt, he really knew he was in trouble. The first receipt was for paint. He wondered "Now, what do I do with this?"

He decided to use his personal money-management software to track all these expenses. He was using the software for his personal finances and figured it ought to work well for *MoviesDoorToDoor.com*, at least for now. He first looked at the software's list of home expenditure categories. He realized that many of these didn't seem to apply to their business. But at this point, he figured the software was better than nothing.

He decided to put the paint costs under the "Repairs and Maintenance" category. As he started looking at other receipts, he was having even more difficulty because he couldn't easily determine why each expenditure had been made. Some of the receipts were from hardware stores, office supply stores, grocery stores, electronics stores, among others. And, the information on the receipts was abbreviated and contained unfamiliar product numbers, making it difficult for John to determine what the receipts represented. As he looked at more of them, he was getting irritated with the entire process. He was beginning to wonder if they could afford an accountant to help them with this mess.

He started to take out his frustration on Brad and Courtney. "You guys need to do a better job labeling the purposes of the expenditures on the receipts. How do you expect me to be able to record anything with the limited information printed on these receipts?"

Brad quickly responded, "You don't have to use that tone with us, John. We're not kids! We didn't think about providing that kind of information given we're not accountants. Would it help for Courtney and me to sit down with you to see if we can remember what each expenditure was for?"

"That would be great," responded John.

* * * * *

To keep the record-keeping simple, John decided to use as few expenditure categories as possible. He put all the expenditures related to fixing up the store in the "Repairs and Maintenance" category. That included the costs of the paint, paint brushes, drop clothes, cleaning supplies, and other disposable items. The costs of the shelving, other fixtures, customer identification cards, and movies went into the "Supplies Expense" category. All the utility deposits and recurring expenses were put into the "Utilities" category, while the lease expense and the computer costs were put in the "Building and Equipment Expense" category. He stuck everything else like lunches, dinners, and the attorney fees in the "Miscellaneous Expense" category. He figured that using these five categories would help keep the record-keeping to a minimum. He didn't want to get this far behind in the record-keeping again.

John was relieved when he entered the last receipt. He had finally caught up. When he was done, he printed the "Income vs. Spending Category Report." He was shocked to see that they had spent nearly $44,000. His stomach turned. How could they have spent this much money so fast? He began to study the report, which showed the following:

Repairs and Maintenance	*$ 1,431.83*
Supplies Expense	*$28,127.72*
Utilities Expense	*$ 650.00*
Building and Equipment Expense	*$ 9,439.56*
Miscellaneous	*$ 4,234.69*
Total	*$43,883.80*

He ran quickly to show it to Brad and Courtney. Their faces said it all. They were stunned to realize that they had already spent almost $44,000, before opening the doors to the business. The $10,000 remaining out of their opening $54,000 was short of their targeted starting cash cushion of $20,000. What would Brad tell his dad when he noticed the significant difference between their cash position and his recommendation?

"Why didn't you tell us this sooner?" asked Brad. "We could have avoided buying so many pizzas and other things had we known we were in this shape."

"Give me a break, Brad. I was busy setting up the computer and related web site," noted John defensively.

"Well, Courtney could have helped, but you wouldn't let her," chimed Brad.

"Enough of this, you guys," noted Courtney. "Let's figure out where all of it went. John, what types of items are included in each of these categories?"

John explained the types of expenditures included in each category. When he was finished, Courtney said "It sure would help if you use more categories so that we could better understand the nature of the expenditures included in each category. For example, the 'Supplies Expenses' category has all kinds of things included in it such as movies, shelving, stationery, among others. I think it would help us to have separate categories to distinguish shelving costs from movies and stationery. Right now, it is hard to see which of these costs exceed our original estimates. If it is stationery and movies, we could be in big trouble."

"Why is that?" asked Brad.

"Well, we will continue buying movies and stationery, while hopefully we won't be needing any more shelving units," answered Courtney. "So, I hope we overspent on shelving and under spent on movies and office supplies. The problem is, we can't determine that with the information we have. If our problem lies with spending too much on movies and supplies, we will need to change our planned expenditures. Remember, we think our recurring monthly expenses will run about $6,600. So, if they actually are going to run higher than that, our $10,000 reserve won't last very long. We may need to find additional funds from alternative sources to help us through the tough times."

John was really annoyed to have to go back and re-categorize expenditures into more detailed categories. But, he agreed to do so.

"Since you didn't like the categories I came up with by myself, help me think through the types of categories we should use," noted John. "It sounds like you want me to have categories for recurring expenses, such as gas and electricity, that are separate from categories for non-recurring expenses, such as costs for the computer and shelving units."

"Well, that's right," answered Courtney. "But, we need to know what we are spending for each type of expenditure. So, that means you shouldn't group too many expenses together. Rather, we need separate categories for each type of expense. For example, we need a category just for electricity and a separate one for gasoline. The more detailed the information you provide, the better we can control and monitor business activities. If, for example, we find that our advertising expenditures are much more than we anticipate, we could use that information to select other less-costly advertising media."

"Wow, you are asking for a lot of categories," commented John. "I'm going to need a lot more information from you about each expenditure so that I can more easily categorize them. You'll need to clearly indicate on the receipts and invoices the exact purpose of the expenditure."

Brad chimed in, "We can do that."

"To make sure I'm breaking this down into enough detail, let's talk through the various kinds of categories we think we'll need," requested John. "Since we have already noted electricity, let's start with that as a category."

After working a while on this, here's what they came up with for expenditures:

Expenditure Categories:
Electricity
Telephone
Internet Access
Water
Natural Gas
Auto Gasoline
Lease Expense
Movie Costs
Shelving and Other Fixtures
Repairs and Maintenance of Building
Office Supplies
Legal Fees
Entertainment
Advertising
Auto Costs
Wage Expenses
Interest Expense

Hardware
Software

Then John noted that they needed categories for their deposits. Here's what they came up with:

Deposits Categories:
Movie Rentals
Movie Sales
Other Receipts

"Thanks guys. Your help has been great. I should have come to you sooner to set this up. I'll go back and re-categorize everything along these new categories," noted John.

* * * * *

After a couple of long nights, John was relieved to finally have a revised report to show Brad and Courtney. He felt pretty good about what he had done, except for the fact that he still had to guess on categories for some of the receipts. Given the brevity of information on some of the receipts, he had to go back to Brad and Courtney to see if they could remember what had been purchased. Unfortunately, for some they couldn't recall a specific purpose for the expenditure. So, John had to add another category, which he labeled as "Miscellaneous Expenses."

To help John record transactions in the future, he created a cover sheet that they would fill out to accompany each deposit.

Expenditure Cover Sheet	
Date:	
Amount:	$
Category:	
Check Number:	
Description:	

He also printed out a new "Income vs. Spending Category Report" using the revised categories to see where most of the money had been spent. The "Income vs. Spending Category Report" showed the following:

Deposits Categories:

Movie Rentals	$ 0.00
Movie Sales	0.00
Other Receipts	0.00

Expenditure Categories:

Electricity	$ 324.00
Telephone	96.63
Internet Access	51.09
Water	100.22
Auto Gasoline	0.00
Lease Expense	3,750.00
Movie Costs	16,840.00
Shelving Equipment, and Other Fixtures	15,244.58
Repairs and Maintenance of Building	1,431.83
Office Supplies	1,312.75
Legal Fees	3,000.00
Entertainment	494.98
Advertising	1,237.72
Auto Costs	0.00
Wage Expenses	0.00
Interest Expense	0.00
Miscellaneous Expenses	0.00
Total	$43,883.80

John gave Brad and Courtney a copy of the "Income vs. Spending Category Report." While they were pleased to see a more detailed breakout of the expenditures across more categories, they still were unsure as to what their recurring monthly costs would be.

Brad noted, "Wow, all the utilities and the lease expense seem high to me. Does this mean we will be spending this much each month on utilities and the lease?"

"No, remember, we had to pay deposits for electricity, telephone, and water. So, those are costs we won't be spending each month. We should receive these back after one year of service, if we aren't delinquent on our payments," answered John. "Our utilities expenditures should be about $350.00 each month. Also, remember that we had to make a deposit exceeding a full month's rent for the building lease. That deposit will not be returned to us until we leave the premises. Our lease payment each month will be $1,500.00."

"What about movies?" asked Courtney. "Didn't we anticipate spending about $14,000 on our initial movie inventory? What's going on there? We've spent almost $17,000."

"Some of the older releases were a bit more expensive than we anticipated," explained John. "And, we didn't anticipate having to pay shipping costs for delivery of the movies to our store. Of course, we are only planning to buy 40 – 45 new movies each month. I anticipate that we will be spending between $3,300 – $3,400 per month on new movies, including shipping costs."

"Well, the good news is that we won't be buying shelving equipment, computer equipment, and we won't be paying for legal fees and paint each month either," responded Brad. "All those expenditures were more than we anticipated."

"Given that we had so much money in our bank account at the start, I didn't think we needed to be too worried about having dinners out and buying pizzas using company cash," commented Courtney. "This has helped me to realize that we need to be extremely careful with how we spend the money, particularly since our parents who invested in this company are going to hold us accountable. I sure wouldn't want to explain why we spent almost $500 for entertainment for ourselves, especially since we now have less cash to keep this business afloat."

"What will we do if we run out of cash?" asked John.

"Well, I guess our next option would be to approach a bank for a loan. I don't think we can go back to our parents for more money," answered Brad.

"If we go to a bank, they're going to want to see our current operating expenditures," noted Courtney. "We want to be able to show them that we are wisely using the cash we have. We need to really monitor our expenditures closely and make better choices about what we are spending our money on."

"I guess you're saying that ordering pizza tonight isn't an option. What a bummer! I'm craving a pepperoni pizza right now," said John. "Apparently, the free-spending days are over."

* * * * *

The three agreed that they would get together once a week to review the "Income vs. Expenditure Category Report." They also agreed that John's newly designed "Expenditure Cover Sheet" made sense and needed to be completed as soon as expenditures occurred so that they would be sure to capture as much information about the expenditure as possible. That kind of detail would help them properly monitor and control their uses of cash.

Discussion Questions

1. What could go wrong if a business did not separate the record-keeping function from the check signing function? Why does it make sense to require two signatures on every check?

2. Brad, Courtney, and John had to spend $3,000 for legal fees to incorporate the business. How should that expenditure be reflected in the company's financial statements?

3. Brad, Courtney, and John created a list of Income and Expenditure categories. What other categories should they include? Which, if any, of their existing categories are too broad?

4. They started with $54,000 in cash before making expenditures totaling $43,883.80. That leaves them $10,116.20 in cash. Other than the cash on hand, what other items do they now own that could generate cash or be sold for cash?

5. Common financial statement elements include assets, liabilities, owners/stockholders equity, revenues, and expenses. Which types of their current expenditures would be considered assets? Which types of their current expenditures would be considered expenses?

6. What are the benefits of classifying business activities into asset, liabilities, owners/stockholders' equity, revenue and expense categories?

7. It appears that Brad, Courtney, and John currently monitor expenditures after they have been incurred. What are the advantages and disadvantages of requiring all three people to approve an expenditure before making the purchase?

8. If you were one of the parents who invested in the business, what kind of information would you want to see on a periodic basis? How often would you like to see that information?

9. How is Brad, Courtney, and John's labor reflected in the "Income versus Expenditure Report?"

10. The computer server is located in the back room of the store in a storage closet. What types of risks does *MoviesDoorToDoor.com* face related to keeping the system running? What types of disaster recovery plans should they develop?

11. Discuss the implications of John and Courtney's relationship for Brad and the business. How might they plan for the relationship growing or ending?

Chapter 5
Rentals At Last

"John, you sure sound tired. Is the new business wearing you down?" asked his mom on the telephone.

"Yeah, I'm tired," responded John. "Working towards our grand opening has been awesome, even though it's keeping me up late at night. I'm amazed at what can be done when you're having fun." He then added, "Earlier today I met with Courtney and Brad to review the financial status of the business. I'll have to admit it was a little depressing."

"Why is that?" asked his mom.

"Well, we ended up spending a lot more than we expected to open our doors. We anticipated using about $34,000 to open the business, which would leave us with a $20,000 cushion for unexpected items as we go forward. We were a little surprised to learn that we've already spent $44,000, leaving us about $10,000 to absorb the negative cash flow we anticipate happening in our first few months of operations."

"How did you spend $44,000 already? You're going to make me worry about my investment now!" moaned his mom.

"If you make statements like that, I'm not going to talk with you anymore about the business," answered John.

"Sorry," responded his mom. "But, remember businesses have to provide information to their owners. Because I'm an owner in your business venture, you can't dodge discussions about the business with me or any other investors. Your venture is just like any other business that has stockholders who have a right to receive information they need to evaluate management's performance. That's one of the disadvantages of seeking cash from outsiders."

"Okay, Mom. I get your point," answered John.

"What kind of information do you have about the uses of cash so far?" asked his mom.

"We have a report that's called the 'Income vs. Expenditure Category Report,' which shows how much we've spent in various categories of business activities," noted John.

"You mean you have an Income Statement?" asked his mom.

"I guess so, but you know I'm not that familiar with accounting terminology. All that we've done is classify each cash expenditure across various categories of business activities," responded John. "The report basically shows where all our money has gone so far. Of course, since we aren't open yet, it doesn't reflect any cash coming in."

"What about the cash provided by the other parents and me? How did you categorize that?" asked his mom.

"Well, I entered the $54,000 we received from the parents in the "Beginning Balance" category," answered John.

"That seems reasonable," responded his mom. "I was afraid you might be treating that as revenue."

"We knew enough to not do that!" responded John.

"If you need an extra set of eyes to look at your information, I'd be happy to help," said his mom.

"Thanks, but I think the three of us have it under control. We looked closely at all the various types of transactions we might have and came up with a game-plan to monitor our expenditures," noted John.

"Okay, just remember I'm available to help," noted his mom. "Before I let you go, can you give me an update on you and Courtney?"

John couldn't believe she wanted to talk about Courtney. He usually tried to avoid discussing his relationships with women. His mom always had fairly strong opinions about the people he dated. He was hoping to avoid her input about Courtney. So, he answered with a short response, "Fine, Mom."

"Can't you tell me a little more than that? How serious are the two of you?" pushed his mom. "Do you think she has long-term potential?"

"I don't know, Mom. All that I know is that we have tons of fun together. You know I'm still young and don't care to settle down with one person. We'll just see how it goes," noted John.

"Well, you need to be careful with that kind of attitude. Remember, Courtney is not only a girlfriend, but she also is your business partner. What happens if the relationship falls apart?" asked his mom.

"I don't want to go down that road with you now. Brad continues to work me over about that. Courtney and I are both mature adults – we can handle whatever happens," responded John.

"Okay, I'll back off. The thing is, I don't know too many couples who have managed to work successfully together on a professional basis. It's extremely difficult. There will be issues that you will eventually need to address. As I'm sure you are beginning to realize, your business relationship with Brad and Courtney can be challenging and complex. Your dating Courtney only adds more to the equation. I'm not opposed to your dating Courtney – she seems to be a great person. I just worry that you'll back yourself into a corner that might be hard to get out of," advised his mom.

"I appreciate your concern for me, Mom. I'll keep you posted as things develop." After a short pause, John said, "I better get off the phone. This is my first night in a while to get decent rest. With this weekend being our grand opening, I need all the sleep I can get. Life will really be busy once we open."

* * * * *

The couple of days before the grand opening were wild. Each day, they rushed out the door of Interconnectivity Inc. to the movie rental store to take care of all the details for the opening, including continual testing of the web site. They were still entering data into the database for the new movies just arriving. They wanted to have all 350 movies entered into the database by opening day. It was going to be close.

They continued testing the functionality of the web site database by logging in from home to make sure it was working properly from a customer perspective. They were really pumped about how the web site looked and were becoming more convinced that customers would see the web site as a unique aspect of their business. Counting on the movie selection search capabilities as their hook for capturing a loyal customer base, they believed now more than ever that the web site would help distinguish *MoviesDoorToDoor.com* from other movie rental stores in the area. No other store provided a sophisticated web interface for customers that could rival having a database of movies like theirs.

The opening weekend turned out to be a little slow. Customers passing by the store stopped in for a quick visit, once they realized *MoviesDoorTo-Door.com* was open. Some of the customers actually decided to rent a few movies, which was exciting. However, Brad, Courtney, and John knew the rental volume would have to grow quickly in order for them to survive. They were encouraged to see that most customers were impressed with the web site selection and ordering capabilities. Most appeared to be fascinated with the ability to identify and reserve movies from home via the Internet.

Over the next several days, they noticed the number of hits to their web site was growing and they received a decent volume of Internet orders for delivery. Most of the orders were for 2 to 3 movies. They knew they had to have that kind of volume for the delivery business to be successful. Otherwise, the costs of delivery on a per movie basis would be too high for them to make money. Apparently, word about the web site was spreading.

* * * * *

The first few weeks following the grand opening provided a real learning experience. Brad, Courtney, and John determined quickly that the time needed to deliver the movies was longer than anticipated. They occasionally got lost as they struggled to learn the ins and outs of several neighborhoods. Orders were coming in from customers living further from the store than expected. The thought of limiting deliveries to customers within a certain distance from the store began to cross their minds. However, they were afraid to discontinue that kind of delivery just yet as they were struggling to build their rental base.

Most nights two people were out on deliveries, while the third person handled the store. It was impossible for any one of the three to take a night off when the store was open. It took all three of them to handle the volume.

While it was exciting to watch the customer volume increase, the three were exhausted. Rushing from Interconnectivity to *MoviesDoorToDoor.com* each day was beginning to take its toll. Each night turned into a late night, which made it especially hard to get out of bed for work each morning.

Working two jobs was more difficult than they anticipated. All three were involved in big projects at Interconnectivity, which demanded additional time. They struggled to keep everything in balance. Colleagues at Interconnectivity were beginning to show some concern, since the three of them weren't as willing to work as late as they had in the past. But, the three felt like they were doing more than their fair share on these projects. They made sure that they didn't waste time socializing with colleagues during the day so they could be as efficient as possible. That, however, was also creating a little friction between them and some of their more social colleagues who talked frequently about their personal lives.

While Brad, Courtney, and John began to contemplate having one of them resign from Interconnectivity to work full time with *MoviesDoorToDoor.com*, they quickly realized from the "Income vs. Expenditure Category Report" that they weren't making enough money to compensate any of them at their current Interconnectivity monthly salary. As a matter of fact, they knew that couldn't occur anytime soon.

In addition to those pressures, Brad was worried about Courtney delivering movies by herself late at night. He was a little surprised to see John's lack of concern. John was obviously more focused on generating business than thinking about Courtney's safety. Brad was trying to convince John to hire additional delivery people to free Courtney from having to make late night deliveries. But, John wasn't ready to hire anyone until they knew they could support the additional costs associated with a new person. So, it looked like they would have to get used to juggling two jobs for a while.

The hardest thing about that reality was they didn't have any free time from work. John and Courtney noticed how little time they had together. Despite working with each other at *MoviesDoorToDoor.com*, they were rarely in the store at the same time. Generally at least one of them was out making deliveries.

Outside of work, there was no time to do anything fun. Brad, too, was beginning to get frustrated about his lack of free time. He had scaled back on his daily running, which concerned him given his goal of preparing for another marathon. He knew he had to find a way to pick up his running mileage, but he just couldn't find the time or energy to get a run in each day. The business was clearly beginning to take its toll on them physically and mentally.

Brad, John, and Courtney occasionally talked about these frustrations and kept reminding each other that these problems were short-term. They all held out hope that it would get better once the rental volume grew to a decent level. Hiring additional help would be more possible once the business reached a sufficient volume to support the additional costs of having employees.

* * * * *

The three of them were encouraged about the business, given the amount of cash and credit card payments they were seeing come in each week. It seemed to them that plenty of cash was coming in the door. Each time they prepared a deposit for the bank, there was a decent amount of cash, numerous personal checks and credit card receipts that took quite a bit of time to process before delivery to the bank.

Somehow the day-to-day processing of customer receipts fell on Courtney's shoulders. She was spending over an hour each night preparing a list of the amounts to be deposited. Customers could pay with cash, personal check, or with a Visa or MasterCard credit card. Customers who ordered movies through the web site generally paid for their rentals at the time of order by charging their credit cards. However, *MoviesDoorToDoor.com* also accepted payment at the point of delivery in the form of cash or check.

It took some time to show each type of payment separately as required by the bank. Courtney had to show the amount of coins and paper currency, and she had to list each personal check on the deposit slip, in addition to listing Visa and MasterCard charges.

She kept telling herself that she needed to do this daily. However, she was so exhausted at the end of each day it was difficult to find the motivation to stay on top of the deposits. Instead of doing it nightly, she was organizing the deposits every three to four days. That helped free up some time. But, when she finally got around to preparing the deposits, the entire process was time consuming.

After each trip to the bank, Courtney gave John the validated deposit slip so that he could record the receipts in their accounting records. The deposit slip served as the source of information to record all movie rentals and sales. John placed the deposit slips into a folder that he used later to record everything.

All the work required for delivery and pickup of movie rentals was keeping John from his record-keeping responsibilities. He fell a week or so behind in entering the expenditures into the computer. Similarly, Brad and Courtney were struggling to find the time needed to select and order new movie releases in addition to updating the database for the new arrivals. In fact, in one of the weeks during the first month they forgot to order any new movie releases. Recently, Brad began helping more with movie ordering and database updates, given the extra time Courtney was having to spend on summarizing cash receipts.

Brad kept wondering why John seemed oblivious to Courtney's need to stay later than everyone else to process the cash received. He was especially surprised to see John's lack of concern about Courtney taking the deposit to the bank late at night for drop off. Brad started waiting around to go with her to make the deposit, because of his concern about her safety.

Brad was growing frustrated with John's insensitivity. He wanted to talk to Courtney about his concerns with John, but felt awkward doing so given Courtney's and John's personal relationship. He decided to remain silent.

A week into the second month of being open, Brad asked John for an updated "Income vs. Expenditure Category Report."

At that point, John responded defensively, "Give me a break! I've been working like a dog on this business and haven't had the time to update the information. Don't forget that you guys failed to order movies one week. We're all busy."

"You're right," responded Brad. "I didn't mean to imply you aren't working hard. I'm just concerned that we haven't been monitoring our cash flow like we need to. We spent a lot more than we realized to open the business. We all agreed that we really need to know where we stand each month. Otherwise, we might find ourselves in big trouble."

"If you can handle the deliveries tonight, I can stay in the store and work on updating the information," noted John. "Hopefully that will allow me to catch up."

"Sounds like a good plan. Let's do it," responded Brad.

* * * * *

John ended up pulling an all-nighter to get the receipts and expenditures entered into their records. He continued to be frustrated with the lack of information available to record the transactions. While the "Expenditure Cover Sheet" he designed provided the necessary information about expenditures, the information being provided about cash receipts was insufficient. Because he only had the deposit slip to record receipts, there was no way he could separate cash received for movie rentals from cash received for movie sales. Since most of the monthly cash came from rentals, he decided to record all receipts in that category. He knew that they would have to figure out a better system for documenting the sources of cash receipts, but he didn't want to take the time to figure that out right now.

Once he had the record-keeping updated, he gave Courtney and Brad a copy of the first month's "Income vs. Expenditure Category Report." They agreed to meet later that night to go over the report.

When they got together, Courtney showed them the bank statement she received from the bank. Her quick glance at the "Income vs. Expenditure Category Report" caught her by surprise. The dollar amounts shown about receipts and disbursements didn't agree with the information on the bank statement. The amount of receipts on John's report were lower than the receipts shown on the bank statement, while the amount of expenditures on John's report were higher than the amount of disbursements reflected on the bank statement.

"I am having a tough time understanding this Income vs. Expenditure Category Report," complained Courtney. "It shows that we generated less cash than what the bank is showing. What's going on?"

"Hey, wait a minute," said John defensively. "All I have done is record transactions based on the information you and Brad gave me. So, if there are any problems, it's not my fault."

While John's defensive tone annoyed Brad, Brad knew that arguing over who was to blame would get them nowhere. "Hang on. There's no need to blame anyone. Let's take a minute to study why they might be different. Courtney, let me see the bank statement," said Brad. "John, did you print the report detailing the transactions for each category?"

"No. But I can do that right now," answered John.

While John was away, Brad commented to Courtney, "Man, John always seems to be on edge these days."

"Yeah, John doesn't handle things very well if he doesn't get much sleep," added Courtney.

Once John returned with the new report, Brad began comparing the deposits listed on the bank statement to the detail of receipts recorded in their records. He found a few cash receipts not reflected in John's report that were listed on the bank statement as deposits. "John, what happened to these deposits - the ones on the bank statement that aren't showing up on our records?"

"Let me see what you're talking about," requested John. After studying it a minute, he responded, "I recorded every deposit slip Courtney gave me. Let me pull out the deposits slips that I have."

John went to the other room to get the deposit slips. As he returned, he browsed through those he found in his files. "I can't find any deposit slips with the same amounts as the ones you noted as being on the bank statement and not on my records. It looks like we might be missing some deposit slips. Courtney, have you forgotten to give me some?" asked John.

"I don't know. Let me think." After pausing for a moment, she responded, "I always work on preparing the deposits at the desk in the back room. Let me go check the drawers to see if any are in there."

Courtney returned a few minutes later looking somewhat embarrassed. She was holding copies of three deposit slips. Apparently, these deposit slips had fallen behind the desk. So, John didn't have them when he updated the records. He agreed to enter those immediately.

"Thank goodness we figured that out," noted Brad. "But, we need to come up with some kind of system to ensure we don't loose deposit information. As our business grows, it won't be as easy to identify problems in our record-keeping system."

"We still need to resolve the discrepancies between the expenditures listed on the 'Income vs. Expenditure Category Report' to the disbursements that were paid by the bank. It looks like we have the opposite problem on the expenditure side. Our report shows more expenditures than what the bank reports," noted Brad.

"Could we have written some checks that haven't cleared the bank, yet?" asked Courtney.

"That could very well be the case," said John. "When I get my bank statements for my personal checking account there are always checks I've written that don't show up as being processed by the bank until the next month. That's why I don't bother reconciling my account. It's always a hassle to keep up with them when I try to balance my records to the bank's records."

"As a new start-up business, we need to reconcile our checking account each month as soon as we possibly can," said Brad. "We're going to be so tight on cash each month, we can't afford to have any surprises in what we think our cash balance might be. We've got to stay on top of it."

They took a few minutes to compare the checks recorded by John to the checks processed by the bank during the month. Other than the monthly bank service charge that was not recorded by John, the only difference between his record of expenditures and the bank's record represented checks that had not yet been processed by the bank. That pleased John.

They were relieved to be able to identify the reasons for the differences between the bank and their records. But, Brad was still pushing for them to come up with a better system for tracking cash receipts to prevent similar problems in the future.

John was becoming annoyed, as he felt that would overly complicate the record-keeping process. He believed it would be sufficient to merely compare their reports to the bank records each month.

"John, why are you being so stubborn about this?" asked Courtney. "What happens if the bank makes a mistake? We might not find that kind of error, without a better system in place to make sure we record every receipt. I agree with Brad that we need to create some kind of record for every receipt we have."

"And, what happens when we hire additional people to help make deliveries and work in the store?" added Brad. "They will be handling cash and checks. We'll need to come up with some kind of system to make sure they don't deliver movies and pocket the cash received from customers without our knowledge."

"Okay, if you want to waste your time doing that, I guess I'll go along with it," responded John. "I don't think we need to worry about people pocketing our cash, given that we will only be hiring trustworthy people."

"John, don't be so naïve," commented Courtney. "Everybody likes to have cash. Most likely employees will be out on deliveries by themselves. So, the temptation to periodically take some of the cash received from customers may be high. We might easily hire someone who is financially strapped for cash. It will be difficult for us to identify their personal financial situation during a job interview. Once they are out on a delivery, they might skim some of the cash and we'll have a hard time detecting that if our accounting system doesn't provide a means for tracking movie deliveries and cash collections."

"There is no way for us to track that type of information with our current web-based customer ordering system," noted John. "We don't have the web site set up to keep track with the number of movies we are delivering. Now we merely use the system to printout orders for delivery, without tracking the total number of movies being delivered. Are you saying that we need to redesign our web site system to capture the number of movies rented each day and track the person making the delivery?"

"Yeah, I think you're on the right track," responded Courtney. "It's too bad we didn't bring in an accountant who understands the types of operating information that should be captured for accounting and control purposes. We are likely to need a lot more information than we're currently capturing to make strategic business decisions. I bet Rebecca thinks we should have the movie rental operating data interface automatically with our record-keeping system. That's too complicated for me to think about right now. All this discussion is jogging my memory about internal controls covered in my college introductory accounting course. It's a little scary I'm remembering that now."

"I wish we thought about those issues and built those features into our system as we created it. Reprogramming the web site now will be hard," said John.

"There's no way we can practically interface these systems at this point," noted Brad. "Let's figure out some quick adjustments we can make to provide summary information on daily movie rentals. We can come up with a way to reconcile information about the number of daily movie rentals to the amount of cash we will be depositing each day."

John and Courtney agreed to look at the source code underlying the web site system to modify it to capture the needed information. They thought they could get that done over the next couple of weeks. John was excited about being able to work closely with Courtney again. Things seemed to be a little edgy between them lately.

Before the meeting broke up, Brad asked John when he would have the accounting information updated to include the unrecorded deposits and service charge. John reacted quickly, "Do I have to do everything?"

"Okay, we are all tired," noted Courtney. "Don't lose your cool. John, surely it won't take you long to record the few deposits and the one service charge."

"I guess you're right. I'll enter the information and print a new 'Income versus Expenditure Category Report' right now," said John.

In a few minutes, John returned with the updated report, "Well, we've got good news. We actually made money our first month."

"You've got to be kidding! You mean we worried about not having a sufficient cash reserve for nothing?" asked Courtney.

"I wouldn't go that far," retorted Brad. "While we made money, the amount was still pretty small. And, you never know how next month will be."

"Yeah, if we have fewer movie rentals than we experienced this month, our $200 cash profit would be quickly wiped away," noted John.

Courtney took a closer look at the "Income versus Expenditure Category Report." After a few minutes, she noticed that the Interest Expense category still had a zero balance. "Wait a minute. What about paying interest to my parents for the loan they gave us? We forgot to pay that. I think the monthly interest expense we owe is about $120, given that we borrowed $18,000 at an annual interest rate of 8 percent."

"Wow, that almost wipes out our entire monthly profit. Do we owe the other parents any interest as well?" asked John.

"No. Remember that Rebecca told us we don't have any obligation to pay our stockholders periodically. That's one of the benefits of financing our business through equity investors. We only have an obligation to pay interest on loans we obtained to finance our cash needs," answered Courtney.

"That doesn't seem fair. Why should your parents get cash while my mom and Brad's parents won't receive anything?" asked John.

"John, we've already talked about this," responded Brad. "Remember, all that we owe Courtney's parents is interest each year and the loan balance at the end of five years. Your mom, on the other hand, has the potential for a much greater return. As our business grows, her investment grows as well. Along the way, we are likely to pay her dividends. Hopefully by the time we sell the business, the stock value will be significantly higher than what she paid us." Brad added, "John, you can be awfully dense sometimes."

"Enough of this," said John. "We've got a business to run. Let's print today's orders and get on the road."

Discussion Questions

1. What are the main differences between an Income Statement and a Statement of Cash Flows? Does the "Income vs. Expenditure Category Report" in this case more closely resemble an Income Statement or a Statement of Cash Flows?

2. What is the difference between accrual basis accounting and cash basis accounting? Which basis is being used to prepare the "Income vs. Expenditure Category Report"?

3. Recall that Brad and John's parents each provided $18,000 as an investment in the business while Courtney's parents provided an $18,000 loan to the business. How would these activities be reflected in the financial statements? Would they be considered assets, liabilities, owners/stockholders' equity, income or expenses?

4. Why do businesses accept payment in the form of checks and credit cards rather than only accept cash as the payment for goods or services? What types of costs are associated with accepting checks and credit cards?

5. Some companies allow customers to receive goods or services and then be billed for payment at a later date. What advantages and disadvantages would exist if *MoviesDoorToDoor.com* allowed customers to order movies for rental and then billed them later for payment?

6. What accounting entries would be made to record cash, check and credit card payments from customers for movie rentals? What accounting entries would be made if they allowed customers to order movies for rental and billed those customers later for payment?

7. What are the benefits to both the company and potential employees of establishing strong policies related to cash collection and recording?

Why is the need for such policies greater when additional employees handle cash than when only Brad, Courtney, and John handle the cash?

8.   Describe how the web site movie ordering system could be designed to ensure that when movies are delivered all cash earned is collected and deposited in the *MoviesDoorToDoor.com* bank account.

9.   Show how Courtney calculated the $120 monthly interest expense owed to her parents.

10.   How does the receipt of cash, checks, or credit card payments for movie rentals or sales affect the following financial statement ratios?
  a.   Current ratio
  b.   Return on equity
  c.   Earnings per share
  d.   Debt to equity

Chapter 6
Becoming the Boss

Courtney couldn't believe it was after midnight when she left the store. As she walked out, she thought, "How much longer can I sustain these kinds of hours?" She was a little frustrated that she and John hadn't gone out together in over two weeks. All their time seemed to be occupied with taking care of business at both Interconnectivity and *MoviesDoorToDoor.com*.

She thought, "I've got to talk to John. We need to figure out a way to carve some personal time for us to do fun things together. I don't want work to be my life, and I want to avoid having another situation like my relationship with Steve where both of us drifted apart. However, given John's defensive nature, I have no clue about how to address this with him."

The next morning, Courtney approached John at work, "Hey, let's do lunch together today."

"I can't. I'm overloaded with work, and I scheduled a run with Brad during lunch today," replied John.

"Okay. How about tomorrow?" asked Courtney.

"I can't tomorrow, but I could the next day. Will that work?" asked John.

"I guess so, if that's the best you can do," responded Courtney.

"What's that supposed to mean? You can't expect me to drop things at the spur of the moment," said John.

"I don't want to get into that now," noted Courtney. "I can see this isn't the best time for us to talk. I'll look forward to at least having lunch with you in a couple of days."

Courtney left John's desk wondering, "What's his deal? It appears that John's interest in me is not his top priority. He seems to be clueless that we aren't spending any quality time together. I can't remember the last time we did something fun. Unfortunately, it doesn't appear to be bothering him. Maybe Brad's dad was on to something when he questioned whether my relationship with John could impact the business. What am I going to do? I really enjoy being with John; however, if he is unwilling to work on finding time for us to be together, this relationship won't last forever."

On the way back to her desk, she ran into Brad in the hallway. "Hey, do you have a second?"

"Of course. I always have time for you," responded Brad.

That brought a smile to Courtney's face. "I'm not quite sure how to ask this, but I'll give it a try. Are you having anytime to work on personal relationships outside of work?"

Brad immediately thought, "She is just like my mother who is always worried about my personal life. Why is everyone so concerned about me?" He then said, "Well, the answer to your question is 'not really.' But, that's just fine with me right now."

"That's not the case for me," responded Courtney.

Brad was relieved to figure out that Courtney wasn't talking about him. "So what are your talking about?" asked Brad.

"I'm frustrated that John and I have had no time together outside of work. The consistent late nights at *MoviesDoorToDoor.com*, in addition to weekends, are running us down and consuming all our time. We haven't had any decent personal time together in a while. And, John seems to be totally oblivious to that fact. I seem to be last on his priority list. As a matter of fact, you rate higher than me, given that you are running with him today," jabbed Courtney.

"That's news to me," responded Brad. "I was planning to get the oil changed in my car during lunch. All the driving related to delivering movies is pilling up my mileage. I can't afford to run my car into the ground since both the business and I need it desperately now."

"Why would John say he's running with you, if he's not?" asked Courtney.

"Maybe he plans to run with me, but hasn't gotten around to setting it up. John often doesn't ask me until the last minute, which drives me a bit crazy," said Brad. "Let's get back to you and John. I know he really likes you, since he talks about you all the time. You've got to remember that John is easily consumed by what he's doing. You know how much our business is occupying his mind."

"That's just the problem," responded Courtney. "I'd like for him to occasionally think about me! Every time I approach him, he seems to shrug off spending time with me. And, he gets defensive anytime I mention my frustrations. What can I do to keep this relationship alive?"

Brad began to think, "Oh, gosh. This is just what I hoped wouldn't happen. How could I be so dumb to think there wouldn't be any conflict between Courtney and John?" He hoped, however, that the problem wasn't serious yet. He definitely wanted to avoid having to exercise the buyout provisions spelled out in their legal documents.

"I'm not sure I'm the right person to talk to about this, especially since I haven't been in a relationship in quite a while," said Brad. He continued, "It seems to me that few relationships are truly equal at any point in time. Sometimes one partner has to work more on the relationship than the other, and that can change over time. It's my hunch that you are going to have to be the driver right now. As long as we are working these long hours, he's going to be distracted. Maybe we need to revisit the idea of bringing in some part- time help."

"I think you're right," noted Courtney. "I can't sustain this. John and I are scheduled to have lunch the day after tomorrow. I'm going to mention this to him then."

"Would it be better for all three of us to discuss this together?" asked Brad.

"Sorry, Brad. You aren't invited! I'm going to preserve that time for just John and me. Otherwise, I won't have any time alone with him for several more days. You're convincing me that I shouldn't bring up work issues at that time. Maybe I won't mention it to him then," noted Courtney.

* * * * *

Courtney couldn't wait to have lunch with John. The more she thought about things, the more she wanted to find a solution to all this craziness. Hiring some additional help seemed to be the most logical answer.

When they finally sat down for lunch, Courtney's first comment was "John, I think we need to hire some additional people to help make movie deliveries. Business has been great over the last few weeks. We're delivering more and more movies each day. That, however, is eating up all our time."

"We knew it would be this way for a while, you know. That's a reality of owning a business, especially in the start-up years," said John.

"Yeah, but I'm not sure all owners of startups try to work two jobs during all their available time. This pace is killing me. I want more to life than just work," responded Courtney.

John immediately thought, "Here she goes again, off on one of her tangents. I'm tired of dealing with her complaints about the workload. She should expect that this is the way it will be for a little while longer. I've got to get her to focus on the big picture. The stress should get better, once the business matures." He then said, "Why are you talking about work here at lunch? I thought you wanted to spend some personal time with me. You're confusing me. Let's not talk about work."

"You're right," said Courtney. "Let's talk about us. Tell me about your run with Brad the other day."

"There's not much to say about it," responded John.

"Was it a good run? How far did you go?" asked Courtney.

After a short pause, he hesitantly responded, "I don't remember."

"Well, I guess Brad will have to tell me," said Courtney.

After a short pause, John said, "I'll confess. Brad and I didn't run that day. I've been struggling with telling you that I had lunch with an old friend."

"And, who would that be?" asked Courtney.

"It was my old college friend, Liza. We haven't had time to get together since she moved to Raleigh. I felt that I had to squeeze in some time with her. I avoided telling you about my lunch with her, given your reaction when you found out she was calling me. She's just an old friend from my MIT days," responded John.

"It's hard to know what bugs me most – the fact you aren't telling me the truth or the fact that you made time for her and not me. As a matter of fact, both things bug me," said Courtney.

"I can understand your frustration with my lying to you. But, your concern about my not making time for you seems odd. We're together all the time either at Interconnectivity or *MoviesDoorToDoor.com*," responded John defensively.

"I'm not talking about merely spending hours together. I agree we are around each other all the time. The issue is spending quality time together. We haven't had much of that lately," answered Courtney. "All we do is work together, which doesn't make our relationship any different than my relationship with Brad. We need to spend more one-on-one time together, if we are going to make this relationship last."

"I don't see us being able to do much of that in the short term. You've got to be patient. I'm sure things will improve in time," noted John.

"Not if we don't do anything about it. I really think we need to hire some additional help," said Courtney.

"That's something we can't decide without Brad. I'm not sure we can afford to bring someone on at this time," responded John.

"Give me a break. You sound like a broken record. You know as well as I do that we are generating a positive cash flow after only four months of being in business. We haven't dipped into our cash reserve since we opened. I think we can afford it now." After a short pause, Courtney continued, "But, you're right. We need to involve Brad in this discussion. Let's just enjoy our lunch for now. I guess we can talk with Brad about this over the weekend."

The rest of lunch was a bit awkward. Neither knew how to resolve the issue, with both on opposite sides of the spectrum. Courtney was dead-set on hiring some help, while John continued to resist.

* * * * *

When Brad, Courtney, and John finally got together over the weekend, Courtney immediately brought the topic up. The more she thought about hiring someone, the more convinced she became that this was the time to do it.

John couldn't believe how she couldn't let go of this. He was hoping her concerns would die down, once she had time to think about it. Obviously, that wasn't the case.

To John's surprise, Brad immediately agreed with Courtney. John couldn't believe that Brad had already tentatively lined up a local college student who was willing to work for $10 an hour. The student could work four hours one day a weekend, and four hours on all weeknights except Fridays. Brad noted that hiring this additional person would cost them $200 a week (20 hours X $10 an hour). So, on average they would have an additional monthly expense of $866.67. He showed him his calculation:

$200 per week X 52 weeks / 12 months = $866.67 per month

Courtney noted that the additional expense could easily be absorbed, since their net change in cash was greater than the expected payroll expense each month.

John quickly reminded them that doing so would continue to postpone the business's ability to pay the three of them anything. There just wouldn't be enough excess cash to cover the new employee and them.

"I hear the government requires a bunch of paperwork related to payroll. Does anybody know anything about that?" asked John.

"No. But, I was going to ask someone in human resources at Interconnectivity," answered Brad.

John responded quickly, "Wait a second. Do we want anyone at Interconnectivity to know our business is doing that well? We don't want them to think we are short timers. We'll end up with all the junk work that no one else wants to do."

Courtney added, "I can talk to Rebecca about payroll related requirements. She'll know the answer and can probably point me in the right direction to get the appropriate forms. Let's not let that hold us up from hiring the student. We need to act now."

John couldn't believe he was letting Brad and Courtney talk him into this. But, it was too late now. He could see there was no turning back. He believed they would have to continue working two jobs for a while longer, since *MoviesDoorToDoor.com* would have less cash available to compensate them on a more full-time basis. They would still need to rely on Interconnectivity to cover their personal living expenses.

* * * * *

A few days later, Brad brought the student worker, Hunter, by to meet Courtney and John. At first John was a bit stand-offish, giving Hunter little of his attention. But, as Hunter started talking about college life, John began to open up to him. John was fascinated as he heard about Hunter's recent e-commerce classes. It quickly took him back to his MIT days. After a while, John began to realize that Hunter was going to make a good fit with them at *MoviesDoorToDoor.com*.

The first weeks of having Hunter's assistance were great. He was taking a real load off their shoulders by delivering movies several nights a week. Brad was able to catch up with the ordering of new movie releases, while Courtney was able to update the database with information about the new releases being added to their stock of movies. She was also having some time to expand the information they were including for each of the movies in stock. John was also able to better manage the record-keeping.

Brad and Courtney were shocked when they heard John say, "How did we ever handle everything before Hunter joined us? He's been a great addition." It was a huge relief for Brad and Courtney to see John pleased with the decision to hire some additional help.

When it came time to pay Hunter at the end of his first two weeks, John was unsure how to handle the withholding of federal and state taxes in order to determine the exact amount Hunter should receive. All John knew was that the amount he received in his paycheck from Interconnectivity was no where close to his full salary amount.

"Hey, Courtney. Have you had a chance to talk with Rebecca about accounting for payroll related expenses?" asked John.

"No, but we're supposed to meet for lunch tomorrow. What exactly do you want me to find out? Maybe it makes sense for you to come along," said Courtney.

"I was planning to run tomorrow during lunch. But, if you think I need to be there, I guess I could attend," noted John.

"Why are you so hesitant? Are you having lunch with Liza again?" asked Courtney sarcastically. After a moment, she apologized, "I'm sorry. That wasn't fair. Every time you tell me you're going to run, I think you're seeing Liza."

"Am I going to pay for my earlier mistake for the rest of my life?" asked John. "I promise that I won't lie to you again."

Feeling bad about her reaction, Courtney commented, "I know that I need to get over it. I guess I need more time."

After a short pause, she went on to say, "Let's get back to the issue at hand. I think it would save a lot of time if you could have lunch with Rebecca and me."

"Okay, just pick a decent restaurant that has a good variety of food. I'm getting tired of all the fast food we've been eating," said John.

* * * * *

John sat impatiently through Rebecca and Courtney's ramblings about their college buddies. Both Rebecca and Courtney shared information about recent engagements, and they both rolled their eyes at some of their friends' dating experiences.

Courtney realized that John wasn't paying them any attention when she saw him checking information on his PalmPilot. "Rebecca, the main reason John and I wanted to meet with you is to get information about how to handle payroll related activities. As I mentioned on the telephone, we recently hired a student to work on a part-time basis to assist us with deliveries of movies. Based on the personal paychecks we receive from Interconnectivity, John and I know that businesses have to withhold some of the wages to cover federal and state income taxes. But, we don't know how much to withhold, and we don't know what to do with that withholding," said Courtney.

Rebecca quickly caught John's attention as she began to explain all the payroll-related taxes. He was surprised to learn that not only were taxes to be withheld from the employee's paycheck, but there were additional taxes that must be paid by *MoviesDoorToDoor.com*.

"Let me get this straight," responded John. "You're telling us that we must withhold money from the employee's pay to cover their portion of federal and state income taxes, based on the withholdings the employee specifies on the government's Form W-4. Plus we need to withhold money to cover their Social Security and Medicare taxes, which I'm used to seeing as FICA and OASDI withholding on my pay-stub from Interconnectivity. What I didn't expect to hear is that *MoviesDoorToDoor.com* also has to pay taxes for employees. Could you explain that to me again?" asked John.

"Sure," responded Rebecca. "While Social Security related taxes are withheld from the employee's pay, businesses are required to match that payment as well. So, in essence the employee and employer share equally in the payment of Social Security taxes. Right now, both the employee and the employer each must pay 7.65% of the gross pay amount."

"You mean that together, Social Security and Medicare related taxes represent 15.3% of an employee's gross pay?" asked John.

"That's correct," responded Rebecca.

"Man, I never realized it was that high," commented John.

"John, that's not all the taxes associated with payroll that *MoviesDoor-ToDoor.com* must pay. In addition to matching the Social Security amount, the business must also pay federal and state unemployment taxes. Fortunately, this is a much smaller amount. Currently, businesses pay a combined federal and state unemployment tax of 6.2% for the first $7,000 of each employee's annual earnings. So, on a worse-case scenario, your business will pay $434 per employee in a given year if that employee earns at least $7,000 that year," answered Rebecca. She showed him her calculations.

$7,000 X 6.2% = $434.00 in unemployment taxes per year

"So, help me figure this out. We'll pay our student worker $866.67 each month. On top of that, we will have to pay an additional 7.65% of that amount to cover Social Security and Medicare taxes, and then another 6.2% to cover federal and state unemployment taxes," recapped John.

"That's right as long as the employee earns $7,000 or less in a year. Once the employee earns more than $7,000, the federal and state unemployment tax of 6.2% goes away," answered Rebecca. "There's also a cap for Social Security; however an employee must earn over $80,000 a year before a business can stop paying that tax, which I'm assuming won't be an issue for *MoviesDoorTo-Door.com* this year."

"Rebecca, what do we do with all the money that we withhold from Hunter's paycheck for all these taxes? Do we get to keep it until the end of the year?" asked John.

"Oh, no. That money has to be remitted to the government on a timely basis," explained Rebecca. "The frequency of the payments to the government depends on the dollar amount owed to the respective government agency. At a minimum, a business has to remit the amounts owed to the government on a quarterly basis. A business also has to file several reports related to payroll taxes on a quarterly basis. For example, businesses must file Forms 940 and 941 to report withholdings related to federal unemployment and Social Security, Medicare and federal income taxes withheld. Similarly, the state requires businesses to file a quarterly wage and tax report. Then, at the end of the year, businesses must provide a form W-2 to each employee showing all salary earned and taxes withheld for that employee for the year. A copy of that form is also sent to the government along with form W-3, which summarizes all that information for all employees."

"The amount of paperwork is unbelievable. It's a good thing that most people don't know about all this when they start their own businesses. Otherwise, they would decide all these headaches aren't worth it. No wonder all businesses need accountants. You need an accountant just to stay out of trouble with the government," noted John.

"I'm glad to see that you find value in working with an accountant," said Rebecca.

"Help me figure out how much Hunter is really costing us," requested John. He pulled out his PalmPilot to calculate the total amount it was going to cost them to pay the student worker on an annual basis. If Hunter worked 20 hours every week, the total annual pay would be $10,400.00.

20 hours per week X 52 weeks a year X $10 per hour = $10,400.00 annual pay

Then, he calculated the payroll-related taxes as follows:

Social Security and Medicare: $10,400.00 X 7.65% = *795.60*
Unemployment: $7,000 X 6.2% = *434.00*
Total Payroll Related Taxes = *$1,229.60*

That meant they would be paying an additional $102.47 each month ($1,229.60 / 12 months) in payroll related taxes over and above the $866.67 they would be paying to Hunter.

That really surprised John. "We thought the costs of hiring a student would be $10.00 an hour. Now, you are helping me realize that our true costs are higher than I expected," said John.

John quickly calculated the additional amount on an hourly basis as follows:

Annual Payroll Taxes: *$1,229.60*

Hours Worked Annually: *1,040 hours (20 hours per week X 52 weeks)*

$1,229.60 / 1,040 hours = $1.1823 per hour payroll tax costs

John couldn't believe that Hunter's true hourly rate was just over $11.18 an hour. "I hope our cash flow will cover these additional payroll related expenses. We never factored them into our decision to hire Hunter at $10 an hour."

"While I didn't expect these additional costs, I think our decision to hire Hunter was a good one," responded Courtney. "Our current volume of movie rentals more than covers the amount we pay Hunter each month. Hunter has also freed all three of us up to handle all the other responsibilities we have at *MoviesDoorToDoor.com*. We were all falling behind on other tasks we have to handle."

"You're probably right. But, if we didn't have to pay for Hunter's time each month, our overall net cash flow would be better," responded John.

"It might be higher or it might be lower. We just don't know. Hunter may be allowing us to deliver more movies than we could without him. On certain nights, two of us plus Hunter are out on deliveries. Before we hired him, only two people could be out on deliveries at the same time. So, now we can make more deliveries each night. In addition, having Hunter frees me up to take more time in the selection and purchase of new movies. If I use this time to make better selections of the more popular movies, we should see an increase in our daily movie rentals because customers will be pleased with the movies we carry," noted Courtney. "So, Hunter may be paying for himself."

"It would be nice if we could measure the benefits of having Hunter on our payroll," noted John. "Of course, that means we need to track more information about what we are doing each month in order to analyze the benefits of hiring additional people."

Rebecca chimed in, "You just hit on another way an accountant can help you. My firm could work with you in designing an information system that not only tracks the costs you are incurring each month, but also captures information on various operating activities. For example, we could design a system that tracks things like the –

- Number of new versus old movies rented
- Number of movies delivered by employees versus the number of movies picked up by customers in the store
- Number of movies delivered per employee per hour worked
- Average miles driven per movie rented or per deliveries made
- Number of rentals per visitor to the *MoviesDoorToDoor.com* web site
- Areas of the *MoviesDoorToDoor.com* web site visited most frequently

And the list could go on. These are just some of the examples of how the information system could be designed to help you better monitor your business activities."

Rebecca continued, "We could also look at ways to provide information that is more forward looking. For example, you could capture data about movies released at the theatres that customers would like to see in your stock. That would help you gain a better sense for your customer demand, which would be very useful in making new movie selections. There are so many ways you could design your information system to help you. To start, we would need to figure out what kinds of information would be most relevant in making business decisions at *MoviesDoorToDoor.com*. I hope this gives you an idea of how other businesses integrate accounting and operational information to make strategic business decisions."

"Wow. That's not the image of a bean counter that I had. The accounting profession sounds much more interesting and dynamic than I originally thought," said John.

"John, accountants provide business advice on much more than payroll taxes," responded Rebecca. "As a matter of fact, providing assistance related to payroll and other taxes is only a small part of my business. We assist businesses as they prepare financial statement information for banks, investors, and others, such as suppliers. And, we provide extensive business advisory services, including merger and acquisition consulting, risk assessment services, and assistance with information technology design and implementation. The accountant is often the right-hand person to senior management for many organizations. As *MoviesDoorToDoor.com* continues to grow, you'll likely want to bring someone on board to work closely with you guys."

"All this sounds great. However, I'm not sure we could afford someone like you right now," said John.

"Our services are not inexpensive," responded Rebecca. "But, if we are doing our job properly, the profits you reap from our advice should more than exceed the costs. The best time for us to provide advice is in the up-front, planning stages. Doing that helps minimize costs associated with retrofitting your information system for the new features."

"I can already see how your suggestions would have been nice to know when we designed our web site," said John. "We were only looking at it from the perspective of the information needs of the customer and not the information needs for business decisions. Some of your suggestions would have been easier to incorporate beforehand. To incorporate them now will be more challenging. As we start looking at redesigning some of the web site, we'll need to bring you in to work with us."

"Just let me know when you are ready. Working with companies like yours on information systems design is rewarding. It's exciting to help a client take a great business concept and make it become a reality," responded Rebecca.

"Thanks so much for your help, Rebecca. We appreciate all this free advice." To change the subject, John said, "Let's at least let you enjoy having lunch on us! Our food is going to get cold if we don't start eating soon."

Discussion Questions

1. *MoviesDoorToDoor.com* is required to withhold a portion of Hunter's salary to cover his portion of federal and state income taxes. How would those withholdings be reflected in the financial statements at the time Hunter is paid each month?

2 . *MoviesDoorToDoor.com* is required to pay federal and state unemployment taxes and Social Security and Medicare taxes. If the company recorded those taxes owed on Hunter's actual payday, how would those costs be reflected in the company's financial statements?

3 . Many companies offer other benefits to employees, such as vacation leave, payment of medical insurance premiums, retirement plans, stock purchase plans, health club dues on behalf of the employee. Why would a company offer these other benefits to employees? How should these benefits be reflected in financial statements?

4. Hunter is paid on an hourly basis. So, there is little direct incentive for him to deliver as many movies as possible. What type of information might *MoviesDoorToDoor.com* capture to evaluate his performance? Describe how they could use that information to create a different compensation plan for him.

5. Sometimes, Hunter may be the only employee at the store. How could they ensure that Hunter doesn't pocket the cash collected from customers who rent movies from the store? Also, how could they be certain that Hunter doesn't let his friends take movies from the store without paying for the rental?

6. At other times, Hunter makes deliveries to customers by himself. How could they ensure that Hunter doesn't pocket the cash collected from customers who rent movies delivered by him?

7. What types of information would *MoviesDoorToDoor.com* need to capture to detect movies that are stolen from the store or never returned to the store?

8. What types of information could be captured to better measure the benefits of hiring Hunter?

9. How would recording the obligation to pay employee wages at the end of a pay period affect these financial statement ratios?
    a. Current ratio
    b. Return on equity
    c. Earnings per share
    d. Debt to equity

Chapter 7
The Celebration

Brad was looking forward to having his dad in Raleigh for a few days. As he drove to the airport to pick him up, Brad kept thinking about how *MoviesDoorToDoor.com* was providing a great opportunity for the two of them to re-connect. Their telephone conversations were becoming more frequent as his dad continued to show interest in Brad's new business venture.

Brad's dad couldn't wait for his plane to arrive in Raleigh. He, too, was enjoying their talks and was proud of Brad's success. He kept thinking about Brad's difficulty in deciding on what to major in at college. Now, it was obvious that Brad's great education was reaping benefits in different ways. Brad's creative skills were definitely paying off in this new business venture. The only real issue they continued to debate was the impact of John and Courtney's relationship on the business.

Brad hated to admit it, but many of the concerns raised by his dad about John and Courtney were also beginning to surface. Brad continued to feel like he was stuck in the middle, often mediating tensions between the two of them. During the first few months of the business, Courtney and John's relationship was rather rocky, to say the least. However, recently things were calm. At the moment, there didn't seem to be a big issue, other than the fact that everyone was still working too hard. The business's growing success was continuing to demand much of their time.

* * * * *

Brad was thrilled to see his dad finally arrive. As they left the airport, his dad updated him on the latest news from home before quickly turning the conversation to the business. "Brad, can you believe your company is already turning a profit after only being in business for eight months?"

"Sometimes it seems like a dream," responded Brad. "Some days we feel like we hit a home run, while on other days we feel like we're living a nightmare. We've never worked so hard. Seeing the rental volume continue to grow keeps us pumped."

"I am definitely impressed with how well you've executed your business concept," commented his dad. "I know it has been tough juggling your job at Interconnectivity with the business startup. But, fortunately you're young enough to have the energy to pull it off. The foundation you're building will likely lead to huge benefits on down the road. Some days I long for being in my 20s – it's an exciting stage of life."

"Dad, your business keeps you extremely challenged, too. It's not like you're in retirement mode yet. I don't see much difference between either of us," responded Brad.

"You're right. But, the excitement of starting a new business is unique. I just want to make sure you guys recognize your accomplishments. You've put yourself in an enviable position at a fairly young age. As a matter of fact, I think we should celebrate. What's the best restaurant in town?" asked his dad.

"I hear there's a great restaurant just outside Chapel Hill. It's pricey, though," responded Brad.

"It'll be my treat. Why don't you check with John and Courtney to see if we could do dinner tomorrow night?" asked his dad.

Brad answered, "First, I need to determine whether our student workers are available to cover the store while we're out for dinner. Business shouldn't be that crazy since it will be a Wednesday night. Now that we have two more college students working for the business in addition to Hunter, the three of us are able to get away at the same time. I'll check to see who's scheduled to work tomorrow night."

* * * * *

Courtney was glad to finally meet Brad's dad at dinner. She was amazed to see how young he looked. "Mr. Johnson, you don't look old enough to have a son Brad's age. What's your secret?"

"Please, call me Spencer," requested his dad.

"Okay, I'll try," responded Courtney.

"As for my secret, I think focusing on a reasonable diet and regular exercise has been the biggest help. While some days it can be a struggle, I still try to workout on most days. It helps distract me from all the craziness at work."

His response hit Courtney pretty hard. She realized that her exercise routine was non-existent. The last few months had been so busy that she cut out her regular workouts to save time. And, she felt like it was beginning to show. Her clothes were feeling tighter.

"Courtney, you ought to check out Spencer's routine," noted John.

Courtney immediately turned red with anger at John's insensitivity. Trying to stay poised, she responded sarcastically, "Thanks John. You look so good yourself."

"At least I'm still running regularly," noted John.

"Yeah, I know. You remind me everyday," said Courtney.

Courtney thought to herself, "I'm going to enjoy this meal tonight, despite what John thinks. I'll think about a diet and exercise program tomorrow. This is too nice of a restaurant to be watching what everyone else is eating."

After they were seated at the table and had placed their orders, conversation turned to business. "John, I understand from Brad that you've been modifying the search engine," commented Spencer.

"Work on the search engine seems to be an endless job. We keep generating new ideas of better ways to capture and provide information for our customers," said John. "They seem to be appreciating what we offer on the web site since traffic on our Internet site continues to expand. I can't believe how many visitors see our site every day. The volume of hits continues to increase each month."

"I think users like the ability to search for movie titles that fit their particular tastes," noted Brad. "As a matter of fact, customer comments received through our feedback section indicate that the search engine is a big selling feature."

"Do you have a sense for how many visitors to the web site end up placing a movie rental order?" asked Spencer.

"We track the number of hits to our web site, and we know how many orders are placed each day," answered John. "We recently started to notice that while our volume of hits continues to increase, the percentage of orders relative to the number of hits seems to be dropping. So, apparently we have a number of people accessing the web site for information who aren't ultimately placing an order."

Courtney added, "We suspect that a number of people visit the site more than once before placing an order. So it is hard to distinguish how many visitors to our site never place an order from visitors who access the site multiple times before placing an order. John has been working on setting up a tracking mechanism to allow us to make that distinction."

"We are hoping that this will allow us to better understand the profile of our web site visitors," said John.

Brad noted, "We recently added a feature to the web site that helps us obtain better information about movies our customers would like to see included in our movie stock. We've incorporated that feedback into our ordering of new movie releases, and feel like our improved movie selection will lead to increased movie rentals."

"Unfortunately, we recently started receiving comments from customers that the response time on our web site can be slow," explained Courtney. "Apparently, some of our customers have experienced brief lags in receiving web site responses to their movie searches. We aren't sure whether those problems are due to the customers' Internet access link or if it is due to our server being overloaded at times with requests. We need to start monitoring our server's usage levels at various times throughout the day."

"That sounds like something you'll want to keep a close eye on," commented Spencer. Changing the subject a bit, he asked, "Hey, how did your last month's results look?"

"Super," responded Brad. "Last month was our best month so far. Our rental revenues were up quite a bit, and some of our expenses were lower than normal. That generated a huge monthly profit."

"Do you have a feel for why your revenues jumped so much?" asked Spencer.

"We think a large part of the increase is due to our recent advertising. We bought more ad space in the newspaper, and we started putting ads in other local publications, such as apartment and real estate guides. Our new permanent signage on the front of the store is helping catch people's attention as they drive through the shopping center," noted John. "We think the added visibility from our sign has helped generate word-of-mouth advertising."

"Don't forget we also started encouraging customers to prepay for movie rentals," added Courtney. "We found that some of our more frequent customers preferred having the ability to set up an account whereby they deposit money in advance of a rental to avoid the hassle of paying each time they rent a movie. To entice customers to set up these accounts, we offered a $0.25 discount per movie for customers choosing this option. The combination of less hassle and a discounted price has been well received. The number of customers setting up these accounts is really taking off."

"Do you know which advertising media is having the greatest impact?" asked Spencer.

"Unfortunately, we don't. John is trying to find a way to capture information from customers as they place an order in our system," answered Brad.

"We are struggling a little bit with the amount of information we request from our customers," responded John. "Several customers have indicated they don't like spending time providing feedback to us. They just want to review the movies and make a selection. We are toying with the idea of giving customers a free movie rental when they provide feedback."

Courtney added, "Unfortunately, we don't think we can afford to do it with every customer. We thought about randomly selecting customers to provide feedback. We would make them eligible to participate in a weekly raffle for ten free movie rentals to entice them to participate. The open feedback section would also remain so customers who are not randomly selected can provide feedback, too."

"Sounds like a great idea," responded Spencer. "So what's the hold-up?"

"Time," responded John. "We continue to come up with new ways to use our web site. I'm having difficulty finding the time to make all the modifications we want. Thank goodness we hired students to help us make movie deliveries. Otherwise, I wouldn't have time to make any modifications."

"I can't believe what I'm hearing," responded Courtney. "John was the most adamant about not hiring help! Now, he's their greatest advocate. My, how the world changes!"

"You think you're funny, don't you," quipped John.

"Well, I'm glad to see you still have time for a little humor. You make a great team," noted Spencer. "Sounds like improving feedback opportunities should be a top priority."

"I know," said John. "It's just that the feedback mechanism we prefer will take a great deal of effort to implement."

Getting the topic back on to the past month's results, Spencer said, "Now, tell me how you cut some of your expenses."

"The biggest help came from our movie vendor," explained Brad. "We've been paying for orders by check each week as we receive the new movies. Just this past month, however, our supplier agreed to start billing us once a month for all movies received that month. Our supplier is willing to do this because of our good payment history and the number of orders we place with them. We're thrilled to have this option because it allows us to cut one check a month to the supplier."

"I'm all for that, given that I record all the transactions each month," commented John. "Now, I'll only have to deal with one invoice per month for all our movie purchases. As a matter of fact, I haven't even seen an invoice for movies we received last month."

"That helped make last month's profits the largest ever, as we didn't have to record any expenses related to movie orders," said Courtney. "Because of our financial performance, we're exploring the possibility of paying a small dividend to our investors. We're paying interest to my parents as required by our loan agreement. So, we thought it would be nice to pay our stockholders to even things up."

"Wait a minute," noted Spencer. "Are you sure you have a sufficient cash balance on hand to cover the unexpected? For example, what happens if your server breaks down? Will you have enough cash to handle repairs or purchase new equipment? Also, how long do you plan to continue using your employees' cars to deliver movies? Don't you think that at some point the business will need to purchase delivery vehicles?"

After a brief period of silence, Brad responded, "You're making some good points. We probably haven't thought this through sufficiently. We're eager to pay our investors a small return. Perhaps, it's a little premature right now."

"I must admit that I'm a little puzzled at how you were able to reduce your expenses. I can see how expenses may be down because you haven't paid for your recent movie purchases. However, it seems to me that you should be seeing an increase in your advertising expenses, given your recent ad campaigns," noted Spencer.

"Last month, our advertising agency made us pay the costs up-front for ads coming out over the next six months," explained John. "So, those costs were reflected in the prior month's report, with none included in the current month's report."

"What about the costs of the new sign in front of the store? How much did that add to your expenses for the month?" asked Spencer.

"We haven't been billed for the new sign, yet. So, that had zero impact on the current month's activities," explained Brad.

"It sounds like you really don't have a good picture of what your true profits were for last month. There are several items that are not being reflected in your current month's report. For example, the costs of your movie purchases and your new sign are excluded. And, you have other expenditures recorded in prior months that will actually benefit you over the next six months. On top of that, you recorded revenues from customers paying in advance for services you haven't provided yet. In the end, you may not have been as profitable as you currently think. Have you shown your monthly records to an accountant?" asked Spencer.

"We talked with an accountant about several issues, such as how to handle payroll, but she hasn't reviewed our monthly reports. We didn't think spending money on an accountant's fees were necessary, yet," noted Brad.

"Be careful," added Spencer. "If you have bad information about your business's performance, you're likely to make poor business decisions. For example, you potentially have less cash coming in over the next few months due to the prepayment of rentals by customers, and you may have more cash going out once you finally receive the bills for the sign and new movies. You better preserve your cash to cover those items. If you don't want to spend money on an accountant, I would at least get an introductory book on accounting to brush up on some of the basics."

"I vaguely remember studying the different methods of accounting in my introductory accounting course in college. I remember that one of the methods was the cash basis of accounting, which is what I think we're using. I can't remember the other commonly used accounting method," said Courtney.

"I think you are referring to the accrual basis of accounting," explained Spencer. "That method requires you to record transactions in the accounting records as they occur, even though cash may not yet be exchanging hands. For your business, I think the accrual method would provide a more accurate picture of what's occurring, given the lag between your business activities and your exchange of cash."

"I wish I hadn't sold my accounting book once I completed my course," said Courtney. "I could really use it now. I never dreamed I'd use the information from that course. I took the course only due to the strong urging of my parents. Now I'm beginning to understand why they pushed me in that direction. I'll try to drop by the campus bookstore later this week to see if I can find an up-to-date edition. Hopefully, reading the book a second time will be easier than the first!"

"We've talked enough about the business," noted Spencer. "We're supposed to be celebrating. Would you mind if I ordered a bottle of champagne for a toast?" asked Spencer.

"Sounds great," noted Brad.

When the champagne arrived, Spencer stood to make a toast. "To my son and his two business partners. I commend you for your entrepreneurial spirit. May your hard work and creativity bring you financial security for a lifetime. Keep up the good work, and don't give up."

"Thanks, Dad. Those were nice comments. However, you're not ready for the speaker's bureau yet!" teased Brad.

Spencer laughed and then asked, "Hey, Courtney and John. Tell me what's going on with the two of you."

John and Courtney were both shocked to hear him say that. They never dreamed Spencer would go there. Neither responded.

Brad jumped in saying, "Let's not go down that road tonight, Dad. I think you are embarrassing all of us."

"I'm just curious. You know I met your mother while working my first job, and that has been one of the best things to ever happen to me. I am thankful each day that we both chose to begin our careers at the same place. Thought I would see if the same thing was developing between John and Courtney," said Spencer.

Courtney's face started to turn red. She had no idea how to respond. John jumped in saying, "There's not much to tell. We really don't know where we're going. We're just enjoying the moment."

John's response really ticked off Courtney. Once again, John seemed to show little sensitivity about their relationship. All Courtney could think was, "Maybe he isn't interested in a long-term relationship." Courtney didn't want to hear any more. To change the subject, she said "Hey, Spencer. Tell me about your exercise program. What's your routine?"

Spencer went on to describe his daily exercise routine. That led to several other topics of conversation. The rest of the evening was relaxing, and they were the last to leave the restaurant. As they left, Courtney and John thanked Spencer for dinner and said goodbye to him since he was leaving the next day.

* * * * *

Over the next week, Courtney took some time to read through the first several chapters of the introductory accounting book she bought. She was beginning to get on John's nerves, given that she kept pointing out areas in their accounting system needing adjustment. He had to make several entries to correct some of the transactions already recorded. He hated backtracking in his record-keeping tasks. He didn't find that work to be much fun.

John's frustration with the accounting software was growing. Because the software he was using was designed for personal record-keeping, John was having some difficulty in reflecting transactions in the manner described by Courtney.

The three of them decided they needed to upgrade their accounting software to one designed for business use. It took John several nights to convert all the records over to the new system. That didn't help his attitude.

One of the biggest issues was how to account for all the movies they had in stock. During the prior months, they reflected the movie purchases as expenses when they paid for them. However, Courtney's reading of the accounting text indicated they should not be expensing the movies each month at the time of payment. Rather, she believed they should be recorded as assets. However, she and John couldn't agree on what asset category was appropriate. Courtney wanted to record them as a long term asset, given the movies would be rented for several years. She felt like it was more appropriate to gradually expense them each year. On the other hand, John thought they should treat them as inventory that would be expensed only once the movies were ultimately sold by *MoviesDoorToDoor.com* after the rental demand dropped off. For the meantime, they decided to continue expensing them as "Movie Costs" until they had a chance to run their questions by Rebecca.

John was beginning to realize they needed to come up with a better system to capture information about purchases already received, but not yet paid. He decided that the easiest way to track purchases was to record them at the point an order was placed. He figured if he recorded purchases then, he was most likely to not miss one. To help him, he asked Courtney and Brad to complete the Expenditure Cover Sheet at the time they placed orders rather than at the time a check was cut for payment. They seemed to be willing to do that.

* * * * *

Later that week, John was surprised when Brad showed up at his cubicle just before lunch. He knew something must be up, given the expression on Brad's face. John's first thought was, "I hope he doesn't want to talk about Courtney and me. I wish he would stay out of our personal business. Brad needs a girlfriend to take his focus off us."

"What's up?" asked John.

"I need to talk with you about Interconnectivity work. Do you have time for lunch?" asked Brad.

"I was planning on running during lunch. Why don't you run with me and we can talk then," suggested John.

"Well, I really need to talk with both you and Courtney together. She's available for lunch. Is there anyway you can reschedule your run for later?" asked Brad.

"I'd rather not. But, if you tell me it's really important, I can make it," said John.

"Well, I think it's important. The sooner we talk, the better," answered Brad.

"Okay. Give me fifteen minutes," responded John.

"Great. I'll go get Courtney and we'll meet you back here," said Brad.

* * * * *

Once they were seated for lunch, John asked, "What's so important that I had to give up my run?"

"Give him a break, John. Can't you think about someone else for a change?" harped Courtney.

"Wow, I can tell you got up on the wrong side of the bed today," teased John.

"Looks like we're all a little edgy today," said Brad. "Maybe this is a bad day to talk."

"No, it's fine. Tell us what's going on," said Courtney.

"Okay. My manager came to me this morning to discuss a new client Interconnectivity obtained in Austin, Texas," explained Brad. "It's a fairly sophisticated assignment, and he wants me to be the group leader for this project. I indicated that I couldn't afford to take an out-of-town assignment right now. But, he quickly pointed out that several other people in my group have already taken extended out-of-town assignments, while I've had not. He clearly signaled I don't have much of a choice, if I value my career with

Interconnectivity. As he left, he told me to think about it for a while, but he needs an answer soon. What do you think?"

There was a long pause, as they each thought through the implications. John started by asking, "How long do you think the project will require you to be gone?"

"At least two weeks, but it could extend to as much as four weeks," answered Brad.

"Wow, that could be a lot of time for you to be away from operations at *MoviesDoorToDoor.com,*" noted Courtney.

"We really don't have any good options," noted John. "If Brad goes to Austin, we'll have to re-allocate our responsibilities and defer activities that can wait until he returns. If you don't go, you may loose your job. And, since everyone knows we are working on this business venture together, there could be implications for Courtney and me as well. It's important for the three of us to show that we are all committed to Interconnectivity, because *MoviesDoorTo-Door.com* can't afford any of us on the payroll yet.

"I guess we really don't have a choice. Brad has got to go," noted Courtney.

"How soon would you leave?" asked John.

"Monday," answered Brad.

"That gives us only five days to get organized for your absence," said Courtney.

"Why does this have to happen now?" John asked in frustration. "Just when everything seems to be getting into a groove, we get thrown a curve."

"Being thrown a curve is a reality for any successful business," said Brad. "Adaptability to change is an important skill for any business owner. I guess this will give us a chance to fine-tune that skill!"

After a few minutes of discussion, Courtney said "I've got to get back to the office for a meeting. We can talk more about this tonight. Hey, when are you flying out on Monday? If you need a ride to the airport, I can drop you off."

* * * * *

Even while on the flight to Austin, Brad began to feel a little guilty. He looked forward to having his nights free from *MoviesDoorToDoor.com*. While he knew the work in Austin would be challenging, at least he could focus on a single assignment. Not having to rush to *MoviesDoorToDoor.com* each night would be refreshing, and spending time in a nice hotel with meals paid on an expense account was appealing.

The first few days in Austin went well. He really hit it off with the client personnel working with him on the project. They were smart, articulate, and witty. And, a couple of them were fairly attractive. When it became obvious that he would need to work through the weekend, two of the client personnel invited him to join them Saturday night to see some of the fun spots in Austin.

Their night out was fun. Brad enjoyed seeing the hot spots in Austin, and couldn't believe the great time he had with Harrison and Maggie. The rapport he was developing with both of them made him feel like they were old friends.

He especially enjoyed hearing Maggie tell silly stories on herself. She really had an ability to put people at ease with her humor. Her ability to laugh at her own mistakes highlighted her confidence. She seemed to know who she was and where she was going.

By the end of the next week, Brad didn't want to leave Austin. His time there had been a good break. While he worked extremely hard, the change of scenery and pace were great. He knew that once he was back in Raleigh, the pressure of catching up on *MoviesDoorToDoor.com* responsibilities would be there. He was already looking forward to his return trip to Austin, which was now scheduled for next month.

When Courtney met Brad at the airport upon his return to Raleigh, it was clear that Brad's two weeks away had taken a toll on Courtney and John. She looked really tired and acted very relieved that Brad was back. Apparently, the business had picked up even more while Brad was away. He didn't know what to say when Courtney expressed her hope that the three of them wouldn't be assigned any more out of town trips for a while. He decided to postpone telling her that he was already scheduled for another trip back to Austin next month.

Discussion Questions

1.   *MoviesDoorToDoor.com* now allows customers to prepay for movie rentals. What accounting entry should be made to record the prepayments? Discuss whether the prepayments should initially be reflected on the Income Statement or the Balance Sheet.

2 .   To entice more customers to prepay for movie rentals, *MoviesDoorToDoor.com* is offering a discount of $.25 per movie rental. How should they account for the discount when customers actually rent a movie? Where in the financial statements would the discount be reflected? Why is it important to reflect the discount in the financial statements rather than record revenues at the net of discount amount only?

3 .   *MoviesDoorToDoor.com's* movie supplier allows them to pay for movies at the end of the month, rather than pay for them as they arrive. What, if anything, should John do to the accounting records when movies are received during a month but no invoice for those movies has arrived by the time he prepares that month's financial statements?

4 .   To help John make sure he doesn't forget to record a purchase, he asked Courtney and Brad to prepare the Expenditure Cover Sheet at the time they place an order, rather than wait until they cut a check for payment of a purchase. John plans to record purchases as orders are placed. What recommendations do you have for John regarding this new policy? When would it be most appropriate to record purchases?

5. *MoviesDoorToDoor.com* prepaid for advertising that will occur over the next six months. Describe how they should record the prepayment of those costs. Which financial statements will reflect those costs at the date of prepayment? What entry, if any, should be made at the end of each month for the next six months to adjust the financial statements to correctly reflect the advertising costs?

6. Up until this point, *MoviesDoorToDoor.com* has been using the cash basis of accounting. Spencer believes that the accrual basis of accounting is more appropriate. Describe the primary difference between these methods when (1) recording revenues and (2) recording expenses.

7. Describe why capturing more information about the number of hits to the web site relative to the number of orders ultimately placed via the web site could be useful for budgeting purposes. Also, why would it be important to have information about the volume of rentals placed via the web site and information about the volume of movies rented by customers visiting the store when preparing next year's budget?

8. How would *MoviesDoorToDoor.com's* costs differ when customers order movies through the web site versus when customers pick up movies in the store?

9. Courtney noted that they are concerned that *MoviesDoorToDoor.com* hasn't paid a dividend to investors, even though they have been paying interest to her parents. Discuss whether the company is fairly treating their investors relative to how they are treating Courtney's parents who loaned the business money. Describe whether the company is violating its legal obligations to stockholders by not paying them a dividend at this point.

10. Courtney and John have differing views as to how they should account for the movies they purchased. Courtney believes the movies should be reflected as property, plant, and equipment, while John believes the movies should be reflected as inventory. Describe how the purchased movies should be recorded in the accounting records.

11. If they record the movies as property, plant, and equipment, how would *MoviesDoorToDoor.com* reflect the costs as expenses over time? What would be a reasonable estimate of the movies' useful lives? If they record the movies as inventory, when would the costs related to those purchases be reflected as expenses on the Income Statement?

12. Brad, Courtney, and John were toying with the idea of using free movies to encourage customers to provide feedback on their web site. What types of information would they need to evaluate the costs and benefits of that kind of promotion?

13. Brad, Courtney, and John chose to expense the costs of buying the movies as they made the purchases. How would their decision affect reporting on the Balance Sheet and Income Statement?

14. How would the collection of prepaid movie rental fees affect these financial ratios:
     a. Current ratio
     b. Return on equity
     c. Earnings per share
     d. Debt to equity

Chapter 8
The Crash!

Business continued to grow throughout the following year, allowing Brad, Courtney, and John to gradually turn over many of the day-to-day responsibilities to new hires. John was quickly becoming more receptive to adding employees who could help handle tasks not requiring significant expertise. Courtney was especially excited when she delegated responsibility for inputting movies to the web site database.

The larger employee base was providing more flexibility for the three of them. They were now able to move away from routine daily demands at *MoviesDoorToDoor.com*, which gave them the opportunity to focus on larger-scale business improvements. One of their biggest projects was expanding the web site to enhance its features, facilitating the ease of use by customers. Obviously, the modifications were being accepted by the marketplace, given the ever-increasing number of hits the web site received each month. Volume really expanded when they got national exposure in *The Wall Street Journal* for their innovative web site. John's ego was bigger than ever, given his heavy involvement in the site's design.

They were finally enjoying their weekends again, often leaving day-to-day tasks to their staff. John and Courtney were finally able to spend some time together outside of work. A couple of recent weekend-long trips seemed to be rekindling their relationship. Courtney was thankful, since at one point last year, she was seriously considering breaking off the relationship as John seemed aloof.

Brad was also relieved to get away from *MoviesDoorToDoor.com* occasionally. He made numerous trips to Texas over the next year, given that his assignment in Austin ended up being much more extensive than originally anticipated. Having a dependable staff took some of the pressure off his being in Austin. Brad felt less guilty about all the time he was away, even though work at Interconnectivity required him to be there. He was finding his time in Texas enjoyable.

* * * * *

When Brad walked into the office at *MoviesDoorToDoor.com* one Tuesday night, he found Courtney and John searching the Internet again as they fine-tuned their plans for an upcoming trip to San Francisco. "Are you guys still working on the details for your trip? How much more planning do you need to do?" asked Brad.

John replied, "We're down to finalizing restaurants in the area we want to visit and to arranging our side trip to the Napa Valley. There's so much to choose from, and we're having a tough time deciding."

"I've got to say, Courtney, that you are the most compulsive planner I know," commented Brad.

Courtney quickly jabbed back, "I'm not compulsive. We're leaving a week from Saturday. If we want to eat at some of the better-known restaurants, we've got to nail down reservations now."

Brad responded, "Oh, I forgot your trip was coming up so soon. Are we okay covering *MoviesDoorToDoor.com* while we're all gone? Don't forget that I'm scheduled to be back in Austin for the next two weeks. So, I'll be out of town the weekend you leave for California. Let's make sure we have enough people scheduled to work that weekend and the following week."

John jumped in, "Come on Brad. You know Courtney better than that. She's had the scheduling taken care of for several days."

Courtney added, "I think every thing is under control. I'll have to admit, however, that I'm a little nervous, since this is the first time all three of us have been out of town at the same time. Hopefully, no major issues will come up while we're gone."

"I'm sure everything will be fine," assured John. "Most of our employees have been working with us for several months. They've seen it all by now and should be able to handle anything that happens."

Courtney noted, "I'm really looking forward to our trip and will try my best to not think about things back here. I don't want anything to ruin this vacation."

"How did it work out this way?" teased Brad. "You guys are going to San Francisco to play while I'm off to Austin to work! I guess someone has to be the mature, working adult around here."

John quickly commented, "It sure doesn't appear that your time in Austin is that miserable. Every time you return, you look rested and relaxed. It must be a good assignment. I'd like to have one like that sometime."

"I must admit, it is one of the best client assignments I've had in quite a while," noted Brad. Wanting to change the subject, he said, "I've got to get some work done around here. I need to order our new movies for the next couple of weeks, since I'll be out of town. If I don't start on this now, I'll be pulling a 'late-nighter' just like the old days."

* * * * *

The next week was a bit crazy as they all prepared to be out of town. Brad was especially busy. He left for Austin on Monday, while John and Courtney were in town until Saturday.

He was excited to be heading back to Texas. Seeing Maggie at the airport when he arrived reminded him of her great looks. He was surprised when Maggie walked up to him and gave him a big hug as he walked off the plane. He thought to himself, "This must be a dream. There's no way someone as beautiful and exciting as Maggie could enjoy being with me."

He knew working this week in Austin would be tough. All he wanted to do was spend time with Maggie. Somehow, he was going to have to focus on his work responsibilities. He couldn't wait for the weekend when they were scheduled to be in the Texas hill country. Maggie's description of the area made it sound enticing. She was quite familiar with it as her parents had owned a lake house there since she was a child.

"Are your parents okay with our joining them this weekend at the lake?" asked Brad.

"Absolutely. My dad loves showing people around. I hope you like horseback riding. It's the best way to see the lay of the land," answered Maggie.

Meanwhile, back in Raleigh things were hectic. John was busy wrapping up a big project at Interconnectivity. On both Tuesday and Wednesday nights, he worked late to finish out some key assignments.

During this time, Courtney was scrambling to readjust the work schedule at *MoviesDoorToDoor.com*. Jason, one of the delivery employees, had to leave town suddenly due to the death of his grandmother. So, Courtney was working hard to fill the gap in the delivery schedule. Courtney was relieved to learn that Jason would be back to work the following Monday. Because of the short notice, she had difficulty filling his time for Thursday night. Her only option was to go with a reduced delivery staff. Thankfully, she was able to find staff who could cover his time for the rest of the weekend.

When Courtney and John left *MoviesDoorToDoor.com* late Wednesday night, John's last words were, "Only two more days of work before we're off to San Francisco."

Courtney gave John a big wink as she, too, was excited about leaving on Saturday. They both knew there were only two more tough days before they'd be on their way.

John noted, "I wonder if Brad is as stressed as we are about being away from the business. There is always so much to do before leaving town. You almost work double-time to cover all the bases while you're gone. So, you really don't get any time off after all!"

"It does seem crazy," responded Courtney. "But, if we're honest with ourselves, it's probably due to our workaholic natures. We could probably leave more things undone than we do. But, it just seems to go against our nature to do so."

"I guess you're right," said John. "Taking care of the details is the only way I'm able to relax while I'm away. It's all worth the hassle - I know it's going to be fun."

* * * * *

John and Courtney both decided to be at *MoviesDoorToDoor.com* on Thursday night because they were short on delivery drivers. Thank goodness they were there since it was turning out to be a crazy night. The predicted rainy weather was apparently encouraging more customers to order movies in advance for the weekend. It looked like the list of movies to be delivered was going to set a record for a single night. Everyone was running at full speed to get everything done.

The telephone seemed to be ringing more than normal with customers placing their orders. Several complained that the response time on the *MoviesDoorToDoor.com* web site was slower than usual. To avoid a wait on-line, customers were calling in their movie orders. John made a mental note to investigate the web site response problems once he was back from his California trip. Things were too busy to deal with that now.

Shortly before 8:00 p.m., John grabbed the ringing telephone ready to take another order. To his surprise, one of their delivery employees, Will, was on the line.

"John, I've been in a car accident," said Will.

"Are you okay?" asked John quickly.

"Yeah, everyone appears to be fine. But, both cars involved in the accident are in bad shape and will have to be towed. Can you come get me?" asked Will.

"Yes, I'll be right there," said John as he hung up the phone.

John's first thought was "When it rains, it pours." Then he went on to say, "Courtney, you're not going to believe this. Will has been in an accident."

"Is he okay?" asked Courtney.

John answered, "He seems to be fine, but needs me to pick him up." After a short pause, he blurted, "I don't know where he is. We hung up so fast from talking that I forgot to get directions. I'll have to call him back on his cell phone."

After a couple of minutes, Courtney asked, "How are we going to handle deliveries this weekend? Will was going to help us cover for Jason. If his car is trashed, he won't be able to make deliveries. What are we going to do?"

John responded as he walked out the door, "I can't think about that now. We'll figure it out when I get back. It might be a while before I return, since Will probably has movies that still need to be delivered."

When John arrived at the accident scene, he was relieved to see Will and the other driver standing as they talked with the police officer. The tow truck drivers were in the process of hooking up the two cars to the trucks. John's first words to Will were, "What a mess. What happened?"

"I was in such a rush to make all my deliveries, that I didn't notice the stop light. I had just glanced down at my list of deliveries when all of a sudden I was spinning sideways. I totally missed the stop light and the other driver plowed into my passenger side. As you can see by looking at my car, I'm fortunate that no one was riding with me. The passenger side is totally crunched," said Will.

"Boy, you are fortunate to walk away with no scratches," commented John.

"No kidding. I'm counting my blessings. Thankfully, the other driver seems to be okay, too," noted Will. "The hardest thing will be telling my Dad, since this car is only three months old. He was willing to buy me a new car, given my great driving record."

"What else do you need to take care of here?" asked John.

"The policeman has already taken statements from me and the other driver and noted that we could leave. I'd like to wait until the tow truck driver leaves with my car," answered Will.

"Should I take you to the hospital to be checked over?" asked John.

"No, I'm fine. But, what should we do about deliveries I haven't made? Customers are going to be really mad that their movies are late," commented Will.

"Don't worry about that," answered John. "I would feel better if you would let me take you to the hospital first. I'll finish the deliveries while you are there and will come back to pick you up. How does that sound?"

"If you insist. But, I really do feel okay," noted Will.

"Let's play it safe and have you checked out. Hop in the car while I get the movies out of your car. There's no reason for you to hang around here waiting on the tow truck driver to remove your car. It's not worth much now, anyway," commented John.

Once John dropped Will off at the emergency room, it took him a little over an hour to make all the deliveries. He explained to customers the reason for the delay. Most were understanding.

The report from the doctors was that Will would be fine. There didn't appear to be any internal injuries. His nerves were just a bit shaken, and he might see a few bruises in the next couple of days. Knowing that *MoviesDoorToDoor.com* would be short of drivers for the weekend, Will was glad for the good report. He wanted to be able to help out some way, even though he wouldn't have a car. He would need all the cash he could earn so he could begin to pay for all the damages.

As John dropped Will off at his apartment, he said, "I'll check on you in the morning. Get some sleep."

John was worn out from the stress of the situation by the time he arrived back at the store. As he walked in, Courtney asked, "How's Will?"

John gave her the good report. Even though Courtney was relieved to hear that Will was fine, she immediately began to focus on how they would handle the weekend. "This means that we have one less person to work this weekend. Both Jason and Will are out for the weekend."

"Not necessarily," responded John.

"What do you mean?" asked Courtney.

"Will indicated that he'd feel up to working this weekend, given that his injuries are minor. The problem, however, is that Will doesn't have a car to make movie deliveries."

"John, let Will have your car. You won't be using it, since we'll be in San Francisco," said Courtney.

"You're car is available, too," jabbed John. "Let him use yours!"

Courtney responded in frustration, "John, you are so protective of your things! You're never willing to let others, including me, use anything you own! In fact, I've never driven your car. You must have had a bad childhood experience."

"Quit bringing up my childhood," responded John angrily. "It has nothing to do with my desire to take care of my possessions. I've worked hard for everything I own and I intend to take care of them."

Courtney came back, "I was taught that material things aren't as important as people. You can be so insensitive."

Clearly they were both stressed by all the events. Growing more frustrated with the situation, Courtney decided to head home. She was finished with what she had to do that night. She grabbed her purse and stood saying, "This discussion won't change your mind. Will can use my car. See you tomorrow." As she walked out the door, Courtney mumbled sarcastically to herself, "I'm really looking forward to this trip now."

* * * * *

John awakened Friday morning still annoyed at Courtney. He decided it would be best for him to keep some distance from her at Interconnectivity during the day, otherwise there might be another blow up. He didn't understand what was so wrong about taking care of things he'd worked hard for. It's not like money grows on trees.

John managed to go the whole day at Interconnectivity without seeing Courtney. When he arrived at *MoviesDoorToDoor.com* on Friday night, she was on the telephone apparently taking more orders from customers.

As she hung up the phone, she said in a frustrated tone, "What's the deal with our server? Our customers keep saying the response time on the web site is too slow. They keep calling in their orders."

John responded defensively, "It's probably the customers' Internet Service Providers (ISPs). You know how ISPs are taking on more customers than their capacity reasonably allows. That over-capacity makes accessing the Internet quickly a problem, especially during high peak traffic times."

"Whatever," said Courtney before answering the telephone again.

* * * * *

A couple of hours later, John decided to head home to finish packing for their trip. Courtney couldn't believe he left without thinking about her needs to pack, too. She thought to herself, "This trip isn't starting off on the right track. Will he ever become more considerate of others?"

Later that night when John was home, his telephone rang just as he finished taking his suitcase downstairs to the car. When he answered, all John heard was Courtney saying, "Get down here now." And then she hung up. Glancing down at his caller ID, he realized she had called using her cell phone, which seemed strange. He was curious as to why she didn't use the *MoviesDoorToDoor.com* phone. John immediately dialed the business phone, but all he got was a busy signal. When he called her cell phone, it rang over to her voice mail. He figured that the volume of calls was high and she needed help taking the orders.

Once he arrived, Courtney yelled, "The server is down. Go check it out to see if you can get it rebooted. This phone is driving me crazy, and our customers are irritated."

John ran back to the computer to see what was going on. After working over an hour, he was able to get it up and running again. Once things seemed to be back online, he checked utilization statistics to get a sense for the number of people accessing their web site. He was shocked when he saw the volume. It had exponentially increased from the prior month when they last checked.

"Courtney, I think I figured out the problem. So many people are trying to access the server that the volume is locking it up," said John.

Courtney quickly replied, "Man, if that's the case, we're in trouble. We can't fix it overnight. The only way to solve that is with more equipment. What are we going to do?"

Before John could answer, the server locked up again. Knowing this wasn't going to be a quick fix, John said to Courtney, "Get Brad on the telephone. See if he can get back to Raleigh first thing in the morning."

Courtney called the hotel in Austin. She was surprised to learn that Brad checked out earlier that day and was not scheduled to return until Monday night. As she hung up the phone, Courtney shouted, "I can't find Brad. The hotel says he checked out today. And, I won't be able to get him at the client because their offices are closed for the weekend."

"See if you can reach him on his cell phone," said John.

"Good idea," responded Courtney. She immediately dialed his number. To her disappointment, all she heard was "The wireless customer is not available."

John and Courtney couldn't think of any other way to reach Brad. They were both puzzled as to where he might have gone. It seemed so unlike Brad to not let them know what he was doing. They thought he was supposed to be working all weekend on his client assignment. They were beginning to panic.

Courtney said, "I'm afraid this problem will continue through tomorrow night. The weather forecast is for heavy rain. So, our customers will be wanting to rent movies for something to do on a Saturday night.

John responded, "We could try to streamline the web site to temporarily deal with the higher usage. For example, we could take away some of the extra features, so that customers will spend less time on the web site. That will reduce the total number of customers using the system at any one point in time. Customers won't be entirely happy with fewer features, but it's better than not being able to log onto the web site at all."

Courtney responded, "That will take some time to fix. I doubt we can modify the web site before our flights leave tomorrow morning. What are we going to do about our trip?"

John responded, "I guess we'll have to cancel our plans. With Brad gone, I don't see how we can leave town with our server down. We've worked too hard to build our customer base to let it all fall apart because of a server crash. We need to make sure this thing is up and running by tomorrow night. If we want to continue offering the web features that we currently have, we'll have to upgrade our server to handle the customer volume accessing the web site. That could get expensive."

"This can't be happening," said Courtney. "I can't believe we have to cancel our vacation plans. We've worked so hard on trying to get away. And, now this happens."

"I know it's frustrating," commented John. But, I can't think of a better alternative. Our web site is critical to our business success - it separates us from our competition. We can't afford to not fix it now."

"You're right," said Courtney.

Then John said, "I need to start working on this right away. Why don't you touch base with the airline while I start messing with the source code? This is going to be a long night."

Courtney noted, "Brad owes us big-time! He's probably off having fun, while we're pulling an all-nighter and canceling our vacation. Wait until he hears from me!"

* * * * *

By late Saturday morning, Courtney and John finally had the web site modified sufficiently to handle current customer usage. They were hopeful that the server wouldn't crash again Saturday night. They were keeping their fingers crossed. Both headed to their apartments to take a short nap. They agreed to meet back at the store later in the afternoon, so they could be around in the event more trouble arose.

Once back at the store that afternoon, they were pleased to learn that the temporary fix was still working. Although a few customers were already complaining about the reduced number of web features, Courtney and John were relieved to see that the server continued to function.

Later that afternoon, Courtney and John were able to spend time searching the Internet for information about server upgrades. They knew they needed a much larger server that could handle a significantly higher volume of customer traffic. Unfortunately, they discovered that the price of such a system was substantial. The package they felt would be most suitable for their needs had a price of $30,086.00.

They were totally depressed about prices being that high. They weren't sure how they could come up with that kind of money to make the purchase. Going back to their parents would not be an option.

For a while they felt hopeless. They were beginning to wonder whether, after all this time and effort, this crash could sink the business. Could this be the beginning of the end?

After staring at each other for while, they continued to brainstorm about possible solutions. All of a sudden, Courtney shouted, "Wait a second. I saw something on one of the supplier web pages about lease options. Maybe we can lease the equipment on a monthly basis to avoid an up-front $30,000 cost."

"That's a great idea," responded John. "Let's check out the details."

They quickly got back on some of the web pages to learn more about lease options. The best deal seemed to involve a lease for 48 months. That kind of lease would require a monthly payment of $830.

Courtney quickly commented, "That's a possibility. Shouldn't we be able to cover a payment like that?"

John answered, "I think so. But, we probably need to prepare another cash flow analysis to know for sure. Man, I hate doing those things."

After initially getting excited about this option, John continued, "Wait a minute. I've heard my mother complain about some of the lease options she was given for medical equipment used in her practice. When I was buying my last car, she warned me that leasing wasn't always the best way to go. Many times it can be better to purchase expensive items using money borrowed from a bank. And, we need to keep in mind that we would have to return the leased server at the end of the lease. To keep it, we would have to pay the fair market value of the server at that time. So, after making all those lease payments, the server still wouldn't be ours."

Courtney responded, "Let's figure out the total cash payments we would make over the life of the lease."

"Okay, let's see," answered John. "The lease length is 48 months and the monthly payment is $830. Assuming this lease doesn't require any up-front payment, we would pay $39,840.00."

48 months X $830 per month = $39,840.00 total lease payments

"Whoa," responded Courtney. "That means we would be paying almost $10,000 extra to lease the equipment. That's a lot of money. Maybe we should check into getting a loan from the bank."

"I think you're right," said John. "At least if we get a loan from the bank, we'll own the equipment by the time the loan is paid off. And, I like that idea."

Courtney responded, "Well, we may not care about owning the equipment at that time. The way technology keeps changing, we may have to replace the equipment before the end of four years."

"That's true," noted John. "I hate to be paying for this thing, if we're no longer using it." After a brief pause, he said, "I just thought of another issue to think about. We may be able to sell our current server to help cover the cost of the new server. How much do you think we could get for our current server?"

Courtney responded, "I doubt we can get much for it, even though it still works. With all the technological changes going on, there aren't many people interested in paying much for old equipment."

John commented, "This decision is getting complicated. I guess we need to get Brad involved before we do anything major."

Courtney responded, "Yeah, if we only knew where he was. We can't wait too long, because our customers may go elsewhere now that the enhanced web features are gone. We'll have to jump on it Monday, regardless of Brad's opinion. This is too critical."

* * * * *

Brad had a fabulous time driving to the lake with Maggie. She let him drive her convertible, which they enjoyed given the gorgeous Friday afternoon. She also brought some great CDs with music from Brad's college days. They had fun listening and singing out loud. It brought back fond memories. And, the countryside was beautiful.

Brad felt like he was in a dream. He couldn't believe how easy it was to talk with Maggie. Their conversations flowed from one topic to another. Many of their thoughts and beliefs were totally in sync. Brad couldn't think of another woman he could talk so easily with, except for Courtney.

Throughout the weekend, Brad was beginning to think that a more-than-friend relationship was developing with Maggie. He wanted the weekend to last forever.

He felt like he better talk with John and Courtney about Maggie before their relationship got too far along. He knew Courtney and John were clueless at this point. He laughed to himself as he thought about this weekend. Too bad, he couldn't touch base with Courtney and John when he returned to Austin on Monday. But, he didn't have a way to locate them in San Francisco.

Discussion Questions

1.   While Will was driving his own car when the accident occurred, what is *MoviesDoorToDoor.com's* responsibility, if any, for any of the damages incurred?

2.   John and Courtney discovered that they could purchase a new server for $30,086. If they leased the equipment, the total amount of lease payments they would make over the life of the lease totaled $39,840. Why would leasing the equipment require more cash outlay than purchasing the equipment with cash?

3.   Using present-value tables, determine the interest rate being used to price the lease payment at $830 per month for 48 months, given today's cost of the server of $30,086.00.

4.   If *MoviesDoorToDoor.com* leases the server, the server must be returned to the supplier at the end of the lease term. The lease notes, however, that *MoviesDoorToDoor.com*, could purchase the server by paying fair market value for the equipment at the end of the lease. How would the fair market value be estimated at that time?

5.   How would they reflect the lease in the financial statements? What financial statement would show the lease?

6.   If *MoviesDoorToDoor.com* purchases the server, the business will be responsible for handling the costs of all repairs and maintenance of the server. How would that differ if the server was leased?

7.   How would the costs of repairs and maintenance related to the server be reflected in the financial statements?

8.   How would the server be reflected in *MoviesDoorToDoor.com's* financial statements if they purchased it? Where would you look in the financial statements to see the costs of the server? Would it be reflected in a current or long-term category in those statements?

9.   When companies purchase equipment, the costs of the equipment are depreciated over the equipment's useful life. What would be an appropriate estimate of the useful life for a computer server? What journal entry would be made to record the depreciation expense for the server?

10.   The server that crashed on Friday night was purchased over a year ago. As a result, some of the costs have already been depreciated. What journal entry would be required, if they decide to discontinue use of the server and decide there is no re-sale value for the computer?

11.   What types of costs would be associated with borrowing money from the bank to purchase the server?

12.   Assuming they were able to purchase the server with cash, how would this transaction affect the following ratios?
    a.   Current ratio
    b.   Return on equity
    c.   Earnings per share
    d.   Debt to equity

Chapter 9
Going to the Bank

It was hard for Brad to return to work on Monday after having such a fun weekend with Maggie at her parent's lake house. Her parents appeared so young and were easy to be around. Brad felt as if he had known them for years.

Because they were having such a great time, Brad and Maggie decided to stay at the lake through Sunday night and drive back to Austin early Monday morning. They both hated to leave the relaxation of the lake.

When they arrived back at the client's offices on Monday, Brad was surprised to find a telephone message from Courtney and John for him to call them at the *MoviesDoorToDoor*.com office. He thought, "They're supposed to be in San Francisco. Surely, they must have better things to do than play jokes on me." He decided not to fall for their trick, and ignored the message.

Just before 10:00 a.m., the receptionist transferred a call to Brad. He was shocked to hear John's voice on the telephone and immediately said, "Why are you up so early?"

John replied, "What do you mean early? It's 11:00 o'clock in the morning."

"I'm confused. Aren't you in San Francisco?" asked Brad.

"No, I'm in Raleigh," responded John. "If you weren't hiding from us this past weekend, you would know why I'm calling."

"I did a little sightseeing this weekend," said Brad defensively. "What's going on?"

"A lot. What do you want to hear about first? Will's wreck or the server crash?" asked John sarcastically.

"What are you talking about?" asked Brad.

"Well, it all started on Thursday night," answered John. "We set a record for movie rental orders that night. In our rush to get them delivered, Will wrecked his car."

"Was he hurt?" asked Brad.

"Fortunately, he's fine, but his car is trashed," answered John.

"That's terrible. But, a car accident shouldn't stop the business. What happened next?" asked Brad.

"Friday night was even crazier," said John. "We had so much activity on our web site that the server crashed. Customers began calling in their orders, which we couldn't handle fast enough."

"Is the server still down?" inquired Brad.

"No," responded John. "But, we did have to temporarily delete some of the web site features to handle the customer volume. That fix seems to be working for the moment. But, customers are complaining about the lack of those features."

"So what's our game-plan going forward?" asked Brad.

"Courtney and I think the only solution is for us to replace the server," responded John.

"That could be expensive," noted Brad. "I don't think we have enough cash to cover a major expenditure like that."

"You're right," answered John. "We think we need to spend about $30,000 to be able to purchase the kind of server that can handle the volume we're expecting to continue. We definitely don't have that kind of money hanging around. Courtney and I identified a couple of options available to us."

"I'm listening," noted Brad. "Tell me what they are."

John responded, "One is to lease the equipment directly from the manufacturer. The other is to buy the server by getting a loan from the bank. The lease terms being offered by the manufacturer don't appear to be as favorable as a loan. So, Courtney and I are leaning towards financing the purchase with the bank. However, we need to get more information from the bank about loan terms before we can make a final determination."

"How soon do you think we need to act on this?" asked Brad.

"We think immediately," responded John. "We hate to loose our customer base, given the amount of time it has taken us to build it up. And, customers are already complaining about the missing web features. So, we think we need to replace the server as soon as possible. As a matter of fact, we have an appointment today with a commercial loan officer at our bank."

"I guess we can't really make a decision until we have the information from the bank," noted Brad.

"With either option, we may need you to come back to Raleigh today or tomorrow to sign loan or lease documents," responded John.

Brad jumped in, "I don't see how I can do that. I have a major deadline for our client this Friday."

"Isn't there someone else who can take over? Aren't you the one running this engagement?" asked John.

"Yes. But, I'm the only one out here this week," answered Brad. "Why do I have to be there to sign papers? You're the financial officer for our company."

"Yeah, but you're the president," noted John. "I assume that whether we lease or buy, someone will need both the president and financial officer to sign the documents."

"Do you think they will consider this to be that big of a transaction to require both signatures?" asked Brad. "When you're talking with everyone, find out who really needs to sign those documents. Maybe they can mail the documents to me overnight if they need my signature."

John and Brad talked a few more minutes before hanging up. John agreed to touch base with him later in the afternoon, after they had more information from the bank.

After he hung up, John went to find Courtney, who was organizing movies on the shelves. "Hey, I just talked with Brad."

"Where has he been?" asked Courtney.

John replied, "He said he went sightseeing this weekend."

"Did you find out where he went?" asked Courtney.

"No. I didn't get around to asking specifics. We jumped right into the reason for my call," noted John.

"What was his reaction?" asked Courtney.

John answered, "He felt that we need more information before we can really decide what action to take."

"I hope you got him to arrange a flight back here to help us with this decision," commented Courtney.

"He can't leave Austin until Friday," noted John.

"What do you mean he can't leave?" asked Courtney who was growing a little frustrated.

"He's the only one out there this week, and there's a big Friday deadline," explained John.

"So we are losing our precious vacation time from Interconnectivity to resolve this issue, and he can't come back here to help us?" inquired Courtney.

"That seems to be how the chips are falling right now," answered John.

"It doesn't seem right that we have to deal with this by ourselves," commented Courtney.

"Let's just find out about the loan option first," said John. "Until then, there isn't much for Brad to do here."

* * * * *

When they arrived at the bank later that day, the commercial loan officer scheduled to meet with them was tied up with another customer. After several minutes of being in the waiting area, Courtney said, "John, quit pacing the floor. You're driving me crazy. Please sit down."

"I don't get it. We scheduled an appointment and they make us wait," responded John. "I hate waiting."

"No kidding," responded Courtney sarcastically. "Your pacing isn't going to speed things up. Try to relax."

Finally, after a half-hour of waiting, Meredith apologized for the delay and invited them into her office.

"So, how can I help you?" inquired Meredith.

John was still perturbed about having to wait. So, Courtney decided to start off the discussion about their need to purchase a new server.

After they provided Meredith with some background information about the *MoviesDoorToDoor.com* business, Meredith began to ask some questions. "Do you have any recent financial statements that you could show me?"

"Sure. I can generate some reports off our accounting software system that shows you information about each account," answered John.

"Do you have a CPA who is involved in preparing your monthly financial statement information?" asked Meredith.

"No. But, we have a CPA who gives us advice occasionally," noted Courtney.

"Hum," noted Meredith. "Who is involved in keeping up with the accounting for business transactions on a day-to-day basis?"

"I do all the accounting," noted John. "We purchased an off-the-shelf accounting package that does what we need."

"What kinds of reports do you generate from this system?" inquired Meredith.

John answered, "The main report we use each month to monitor our business is an Income Statement generated automatically by our accounting software system. It summarizes cash receipts and cash disbursements we've had for the month. We also print out a Check Register, which shows our running cash balance."

Meredith responded, "Before the loan can be approved, I'll need to see the most recent corporate tax returns along with the last twelve monthly Income Statement reports. I will also need a listing of all your assets and any obligations to vendors or any other third parties you might owe. All this information is required to meet our bank's lending policy. We use it to help assess your ability to meet the loan obligation."

Courtney turned to John, "How long do you think it will take us to get that information pulled together?"

John answered, "Everything should be pretty straight-forward, except for the listing of assets. We haven't really been keeping track of that. This could take a couple of days."

"Give me what you have ready now, so that we can start processing the loan," noted Meredith. "You can forward me the other information as soon as you have it pulled together."

"I can fax you a lot of this information later this afternoon," responded John.

"That's great," commented Meredith. "Now, let's think a little bit more about your long-term plans. Do you anticipate any additional financing needs in the next year or two?"

Courtney responded, "We've been thinking about expanding to other locations in the city. We'll need some additional cash to open up another store stocked with videos and DVDs. Why do you ask about this now?"

Meredith explained, "It might make sense to consider opening up a line of credit, in addition to the loan for the server. How much did it take to open your current store?"

"We used about $50,000 to open the doors," responded John. "We'd like to open three or four new locations in the next couple of years. So, our total cash needs could approach $200,000."

"If you really think you'll expand in the near future, you may want to consider having a CPA assist you in preparing more formal financial statements prepared in accordance with generally accepted accounting principles," explained Meredith.

"Why is that?" asked John.

Meredith responded, "As your loan balance increases, there is more potential risk for a lender. As a result, a lender wants better information to evaluate the credit worthiness of the business. We're used to looking at Balance Sheets, Income Statements, and Statements of Cash Flows prepared in accordance with standard accounting principles. They provide a nice overview of the past financial performance of a business. They help us in assessing a company's ability to meet future loan payment obligations. Obviously, a company's business plan is most important. Based on what I'm hearing, it seems like your strategy has been successful so far."

They discussed their potential long-term financing needs a bit further, but decided that the most important thing to accomplish at the moment was processing the loan for the new server. They all agreed that they could focus on the line of credit and other financing options at a later date.

As they were leaving the bank, John complained to Courtney, "It sure seems like they are making us go through a bunch of busy work just to get this loan approved. They provide us monthly bank statements for our checking account that show the cash receipts and disbursements we have each month. Doesn't that provide them enough information about how our business is doing? Why are they making us jump through all these hoops? I thought banks were getting more user friendly."

Courtney responded, "The bank statements don't show the context of any of those receipts and disbursements. There is no information about the sources of the receipts and how we use the cash. Banks are in the business of loaning money. Banks don't want to give out money that they will eventually lose. I would want a lot more information if I was going to be lending money to someone I don't know."

"Why do they need information about our assets and liabilities?" asked John.

"Well, its probably the same issue you see when you try to get a car loan," responded Courtney. "A bank is willing to loan money for the purchase of a car, because they know that if the borrower doesn't repay the loan the bank will at least get the car, which can later be sold to pay off the loan. My guess is that Meredith probably wants to see a list of our assets so she can determine what might be available to the bank in the event we don't repay the loan."

"Okay. But, what about the liabilities?" asked John.

Courtney answered, "That's a little tougher to understand. But, she probably wants to see what claims other lenders have to our assets. If a company's liabilities are about equal to the company's assets, there may not be any cash available should the company not repay a bank loan. Also, the bank may want to see the extent a company has other liabilities to assess the company's ability to meet short-term and long-term cash obligations. That helps the bank determine whether a business can handle another monthly payment, based on the current cash coming in and going out each month."

"Well, I don't like having to get all this information together for them," moaned John. "It's taking our attention away from running our business."

"Well, our business won't be worth much if we don't get this loan," responded Courtney. "We can't survive if we're unable to get the new server."

As they got in the car, John said, "Help me think about what kinds of assets we have."

"Well, we have some cash in the bank, and we have a huge stock of videos and DVDs," responded Courtney.

"Okay, that makes sense," responded John. "Now, help me think about our liabilities."

"The biggest liability we have is the loan to my parents," answered Courtney. "We may also have an invoice or two from our movie suppliers who bill us monthly for new movie purchases. Other than those items, I really can't think of any other liabilities."

"What about the money from my mom and Brad's parents?" asked John.

"John, you keep forgetting that your mom and Brad's parents didn't lend us money," Courtney responded in frustration.

"Why not?" asked John. "My mom wants a return on her investment just like your parents want one, too."

"How many times do we have to go through this?" complained Courtney. "Your mom is a stockholder, not a lender. She'll get money if the stock is ever sold or if we liquidate the company and sell off the assets on behalf of the stockholders."

"Yeah, but she may not get the full amount she invested," said John. "In contrast, you keep telling me that in five years your parents will get back the full amount they loaned us."

"You're right," commented Courtney. "But, if the business stays strong, your mom has the potential to get back significantly more than she invested. Those are some of the risks and benefits of being a stockholder. My parents, however, are locked into receiving a return of only 8 percent per year. They don't get to share in the success of our company beyond an 8 percent annual return. So, while they bear less risk, they receive a smaller benefit in return."

"Okay, I remember we've talked about this before," responded John. After a few minutes, John said, "Coming up with an amount for the liabilities shouldn't be too difficult using our current records. But, we never resolved the issue of how we should handle movies. Should I show our movies at the amount we paid when we originally bought them from the vendor? Or, do I show them at the price we sell them for once they aren't used for rental purposes? You know, there is a big difference in those two amounts."

Courtney answered, "John, don't you remember my telling you that we are supposed to show long-term assets based on their original purchase price reduced by some estimate reflecting their usage over time."

"I guess I'm all for that now, since it gives us a higher value to show for our assets," responded John. "That will present the prettiest picture to the bank."

* * * * *

Once they got back to the *MoviesDoorToDoor.com* office, John pulled together the already available information requested by Meredith. After faxing that to her, he began working on the schedule of assets and liabilities. He began by trying to determine the original invoice price for each movie currently in stock. After a while, he realized this approach would take a long time to complete. He commented to Courtney, "The approach I'm using to value the video and DVD stock is taking too much time."

Courtney responded, "Tell me what you're doing."

"I'm going to the original invoices to determine the price we paid for each video and DVD we have in stock," explained John. "But, we have a lot of movies now. This is going to take me forever to complete."

"Couldn't we just compute an average price per movie by using each month's Income Statement report?" asked Courtney. "That report has a separate line item labeled 'Movie Costs' that we could use to compute some kind of average. We could add the monthly amount from that line item for each month since we have been in business to calculate the total amount we've paid for all our movies."

"Brilliant idea," responded John. After a short pause, he said, "Wait a second. What do we do about the movies we've sold since then?"

"Oh, you're right," noted Courtney. "I guess we need to back out the purchase price of movies we've sold."

"How are we going to do that?" asked John.

Courtney answered, "Well, we could go back and pull the invoices for the movies we sold. But, that could take a while. Maybe another approach is to just count up the number of movies we have sold each month, using information from the Income Statement. We could add the number of movies we've sold to the number of movies we currently have in stock. The grand total would represent the total number of movies we have purchased since opening our doors. Then we could divide the total number of movies into the total dollar amount from the 'Movie Costs' line in the Income Statement Reports we've generated since we started. That would give us an average cost per movie. We can multiply that average cost per movie times the number of movies we currently have in stock to get an estimate of the value for movies currently on hand."

John responded, "That will take some time, but it will be faster than what I was doing. I'm going to get started on using your suggested approach right now.

* * * * *

Courtney's suggestion worked well. John was pleased that he was able to get an estimate of the value of their movie stock by the end of the day. Valuing the other assets and the liabilities went smoothly. He was able to fax the rest of the information to Meredith by early the next morning, which was ahead of schedule.

Later that next day, Meredith called to tell Courtney and John that the loan was approved. The bank was willing to lend money for the server under a 48 month installment note at 8 1/8 percent interest annually, which would require a monthly payment of $736.26. Meredith also noted that the loan was contingent on *MoviesDoorToDoor.com*'s willingness to use the server and the movie inventory as collateral for the loan.

During their phone conversation, Meredith also pointed out a perceived inconsistency in the way *MoviesDoorToDoor.com* was accounting for the costs of movie purchases. She explained that the Schedule of Assets prepared by John included all the movies currently in stock as assets, while the corporate tax returns included the costs of movies purchased during each year as expenses. Although the apparent inconsistency didn't affect the bank's loan decision, Meredith suggested that they talk with an accountant to determine the appropriate method for reflecting movie costs in their accounting records. John made a mental note to give Rebecca a call.

Other than that, all that Courtney and John needed to do was come into the bank to sign the loan agreement. John asked if Brad had to sign the papers. Meredith indicated that the bank was comfortable with having just Courtney's and John's signatures, since they both were officers of the company. It wouldn't be necessary for this loan to have Brad's signature.

When they got off the phone with Meredith, John quickly calculated the total amount of loan payments they would make over the life of the loan. He figured that by the end of the 48 months, *MoviesDoorToDoor.com* would pay $35,340.48.

$$\$736.26 \ X \ 48 \ months = \$35,340.48$$

John quickly commented, "Wow, that's a lot better deal than the lease option offered by the server's manufacturer. Remember, the lease required a $830 monthly payment. Plus we will have full title to the equipment after the loan is paid."

"It seems obvious to me that the loan makes the best sense," responded Courtney. "But, we still need to call Brad. I'm sure he'll agree with us."

"Let's call him now. We need to resolve this so we can get the server up and running," noted John.

"Let me do the talking," said Courtney. "I want to find out where he was this past weekend. I know you won't ask. Give me the phone number."

Brad answered the phone after two rings. Courtney immediately said, "Thank goodness you're there. We need to fill you in on the financing options related to the purchase of the new server. Yesterday, we met with the commercial loan officer from our bank. Before she could make a loan decision, we needed to pull together more financial information."

"What kind of stuff did she need?" asked Brad.

"In addition to the monthly reports we generate, she wanted a listing of all of our assets and liabilities and copies of our tax returns. It took John the rest of yesterday and part of this morning to pull together the information, since we hadn't really maintained records on those items. Fortunately, the commercial loan officer was able to meet with the bank's loan committee today and they approved the loan to us."

"That's great!" commented Brad. "How do the loan terms compare to the lease terms?"

"Well, the length of the loan is 48 months just like the lease. The basic difference is that we would pay $830 monthly if we lease the equipment but only $736 a month if we borrow the money from the bank," explained Courtney.

"Wow, that's big a difference," responded Brad. "That will save us about $100 a month, which translates into a savings of $4,800 over the life of the loan. Based on that, I guess we have to go with the loan. Are you aware of any other differences we should consider? Given the big difference in payments, I wonder if there is some issue related to the two financing arrangements that we aren't thinking about. "

"Like what?" asked Courtney.

"What happens if we decide we need a better server in two years before the loan or lease expire?" asked Brad. "I wonder if it is easier to upgrade to a newer server if we go with a lease from the manufacturer?"

"I have no idea," responded Courtney. "We would need to check the lease terms for a lease cancellation option. But, it seems to me that we would be paying quite a bit of extra money to have that kind of flexibility. It doesn't seem worth it to me."

Brad asked, "What does John think about our options?"

"Hold on a second, let me update him on your concern first," noted Courtney.

After a few seconds, Courtney was back on the phone. "John still thinks the loan makes the best sense."

"Ok, let's go for it," answered Brad. "I appreciate your taking vacation time to take care of these problems. I know it's been a bummer to not be in San Francisco this week."

"That reminds me. Where were you this past weekend?" asked Courtney.

"I did some sightseeing in the area," answered Brad. "I've been coming down here for a year without seeing anything. I figured I should get to know the area," answered Brad.

"You did that by yourself?" asked Courtney.

"No. Someone from the client showed me around," responded Brad.

"Male or female?" asked Courtney.

"What difference does that make?" asked Brad.

"Just answer the question. Male or female?" demanded Courtney.

"It was a female!" responded Brad. "Does that make you happy? I can't talk anymore. My client is waiting on me for a meeting."

"Don't think we're dropping this one. I'll have a lot more questions when you return to Raleigh. By the way, when will you be back?" asked Courtney.

"Late on Friday," quipped Brad. "I really do need to go. They're waiting on me now. Bye."

After Courtney hung up the phone, she quickly turned to John. "You'd never believe this. Brad did some sightseeing this weekend with a woman. His short responses suggests there's got to be something going on."

"Hard for me to believe there's much to it," commented John. "I've watched him around women before and he doesn't handle those situations very well. I'd be surprised if there's a romantic relationship going on in Austin."

"I don't know. I have a funny feeling about his. I'll grill him with questions when he gets back," noted Courtney. "In the meantime, we need to touch base with Meredith so that we can sign the loan papers this afternoon."

"I'll call her now," said John. "I want to take care of this quickly. That will allow us to place the order for the server this afternoon.

* * * * *

When Brad hung up the phone, he turned and smiled embarrassingly at Maggie. She quickly noted, "That sure was a short conversation."

"Yeah. Courtney and John were surprised that they couldn't locate me this past weekend and wanted to know what was going on," explained Brad. "And, I really didn't want to get into that now."

"Well, what was going on this weekend?" asked Maggie.

"Some sightseeing in the Texas hill country with good company," responded Brad.

"Just good company?" asked Maggie hesitantly.

After a brief pause, Brad responded "No. Actually, fantastic company,"

At that point, their eyes connected and an affectionate smile came across both their faces.

* * * * *

Over the next couple of days, Courtney and John closed on the loan, ordered the server, and continued patch-working the web site to keep it up and running while they waited for the new server to arrive. Although they would have preferred going to San Francisco, they were especially glad the crash occurred when they were scheduled to be away from Interconnectivity. Taking care of all the problems was occupying most of their time.

Things seemed to be getting back on track by Thursday. John was busy working on the web site when the phone rang. When he answered it, the voice on the other end introduced himself as Dan Archer.

"I am trying to reach Brad Johnson, who I understand is the president of *MoviesDoorToDoor.com*," said Mr. Archer.

"I'm sorry, but he's not here. As a matter of fact, he is traveling this week," responded John. "Perhaps, I can help you. I'm the financial officer of the company."

"I am representing Will Morgan, who I'm sure you know is one of your employees," commented Mr. Archer.

"Of course I know him," quickly responded John. "Why does he need legal representation? I saw him yesterday here at work, and he looked fine to me."

"As you may be aware, Will was involved in a car accident last week while he was delivering movies for your company. The individual in the other car is now claiming to be injured. I've been informed by their attorney that they intend to file a lawsuit if a reasonable settlement cannot be worked out. Since Will's accident occurred while he was at work, *MoviesDoorToDoor.com* has a legal obligation to pay the damages."

"What do you mean?" asked John. "We didn't cause Will's accident. He was the one driving carelessly. So, why should our company owe anything?"

"Since Will was performing his work responsibilities, he was representing your company at the time of the accident. I think it is in everybody's best interest for all of us to come up with a reasonable settlement," commented Mr. Archer.

"What is the other party asking for?" questioned John.

"The injured party wants full replacement of their car, plus coverage of all medical expenses and lost pay while away from work. At this point, the injured party hasn't discussed any compensation for pain and suffering. I anticipate that if this case goes to court, they'll add that as an additional claim in the case," explained Mr. Archer.

"No offense to you, but you sure are ruining my day, Mr. Archer," responded John. "Obviously, I need to contact my attorney. Can you give me your phone number so that either my attorney or I can contact you?"

"Sure. Would you like me to contact your attorney directly?" asked Mr. Archer.

"Garrett Hayley is our attorney," noted John. "I would prefer to contact him first, though."

"I understand. I'll follow-up with you in a couple of days, if I haven't heard from you or Mr. Hayley," explained Mr. Archer. He then gave John the contact information.

When John hung up the telephone, he sat frozen for a moment. He kept thinking, "What else could go wrong? All our hard work could be for nothing the way things are going right now. What will Courtney and Brad think?"

Discussion Questions

1.   While driving from the bank, Courtney and John listed the assets and liabilities to be included on the schedule that they will prepare for the bank. What other assets and liabilities have they failed to consider?

2.   Because the movies in the store would be classified as property, plant, and equipment, is it appropriate to show the movies on his schedule of assets and liabilities to be given to the bank using the original purchase price for the movies? Explain your answer.

3.   What risk, if any, would Brad, Courtney, and John bear if they exclude known liabilities from the information they present to the bank?

4.   Given that they decided to purchase the server by borrowing money from the bank, how would that transaction be reflected on the company's financial statements?

5.   Assume that *MoviesDoorToDoor.com* decided to lease the server rather than purchase it. How would the lease transaction be reflected in the company's financial statements?

6.   Both the lease option and the loan from the bank required monthly payments over a 48-month time frame. And, the amount they would borrow from the bank equals the price of the equipment they would lease ($30,086). So, why is there a difference in the monthly loan payment amount and the monthly lease payment amount?

7.   *MoviesDoorToDoor.com* could purchase the server by entering into a lease with the server manufacturer or they could borrow the money from a bank. The manufacturer of the computer server runs a risk that *MoviesDoorToDoor.com* might default on the lease payments. The bank bears a similar risk if they loan money to *MoviesDoorTo-Door.com*. How could the server manufacturer's risk of customer defaults on leases differ from the default risks banks have when they loan money to customers for a variety of purchases?

8.   Why would the bank be interested in reviewing *MoviesDoorTo-Door.com's* tax returns if they already had information about the business through the Income Statement generated by John?

9.   How should *MoviesDoorToDoor.com's* financial statements reflect the potential lawsuit associated with Will's car accident?

10.   How should *MoviesDoorToDoor.com* handle explaining the lawsuit situation to the bank, given that the loan was already approved and the loan paper work was completed?

11.   Brad, Courtney, and John have not received any compensation from *MoviesDoorToDoor.com*. How is all their work reflected in the financial information submitted to the bank?

12.   Since *MoviesDoorToDoor.com* is not generating sufficient cash to give Brad, Courtney, or John a salary, how else could they be compensated for their efforts?

Chapter 10
Getting Smart – Tapping
the Market

Brad's recent time in Austin had been unbelievable for him. Having the chance to be with Maggie on a day-to-day basis at work was great. The weekend in the hill country was a definite highlight, too. Brad felt like Maggie was enjoying his being there just as much.

Just before Brad prepared to leave Austin to return to Raleigh, the client's chief technology officer, Cara King, called Brad to her office. Brad expected her to thank him for his work there in Austin, since things had gone relatively well. To his surprise, Cara made Brad a full-time offer to join the company's information technology division. The financial package was unbelievable and the thought of working with Maggie was enticing. But, he couldn't figure out how he could make it work given his involvement with *MoviesDoorTo-Door.com*. He left the conversation with Cara by asking how long she could wait for his response. Fortunately, she graciously noted that he could take as long as he needed. Brad, however, knew that didn't mean forever.

Once he left Cara's office, he started to gather his things so he could head to the airport. While packing, the thought, "So much is happening to me right now," kept racing across his mind. He wondered, "Should I tell Maggie about the offer? Am I ready to move to Austin? If I do, how will Maggie react? What should I say to Courtney and John? What do I do about my job at Interconnectivity? How could I get out of my responsibilities at *MoviesDoor-ToDoor.com*?" It was difficult for him to maintain focus.

Maggie startled Brad when she walked in the room to see if he was ready to go to the airport. "Give me a couple of minutes. I'm almost done," responded Brad.

When he left the client's building, Brad wondered if he would ever be back there again. This last trip to Austin was to wrap-up the final phase of the consulting engagement. The two weeks went as expected, so there was no plan for him to come back there on Interconnectivity's behalf.

As Maggie drove him to the airport, Brad didn't say much. Questions kept rolling across his mind, "Are my feelings for Maggie real? She seems to be interested in me, but what if I'm wrong? Is it time for me to expose my feelings for her?"

Maggie was quiet, too. She hated the thought of Brad leaving Austin with no scheduled return. She kept wishing Brad would initiate conversation about them. But, he seemed to be in his own world listening to the radio.

When they arrived at the airport, Maggie decided to park the car and walk with Brad to the gate, so that they could spend more time together. She kept hoping he would say something about them.

Brad finally decided that he would show his feelings for her by giving her a kiss when he left to board the plane. When they arrived at the gate, the seating area was packed with people. So, they decided to stand by the gate door. As Brad's flight was called for boarding, his nervousness began to overwhelm him. He went into panic mode, only able to give her a hug before heading to the plane.

As he walked away, Maggie realized he wasn't going to say anything. So, she called for him. "Brad, I want you to know that I've really enjoyed getting to know you over the past several months. I hope we stay in touch. You're always welcome in Austin."

"I've had a blast as well," responded Brad quickly. "You can count on hearing from me soon." They made the last call for boarders, so Brad had to leave. As he went through the gate doorway, he turned to wave goodbye to Maggie. He thought to himself as he walked down the corridor to the plane, "You wimp. You didn't let her know how you feel."

Maggie was sad as she left the gate area. She would miss Brad terribly and wondered if she would ever see him again. She realized that she had fallen for him. While she was frustrated with Brad's lack of communication about them, his shyness and respect for their friendship was endearing.

On the flight back to Raleigh, the reality of being separated from Maggie was beginning to hit him hard. He couldn't remember having a relationship like this. He wondered what she would think about his job offer in Austin. "What am I going to do?" he kept wondering. Needless to say, the flight back wasn't restful.

* * * * *

Brad, Courtney, and John arranged to meet first thing Saturday morning at *MoviesDoorToDoor.com*. So much had been going on. When he arrived, Brad was surprised to see how tired both Courtney and John appeared. He commented sarcastically, "How was your vacation?"

"That's not funny," responded Courtney. "This past week was rough. Thank goodness John and I did have vacation time scheduled. We've been working all kinds of hours to keep this place up and running."

"You're right. I appreciate what you guys have done," noted Brad. "How is the new server working?"

John laughed out of frustration and then said, "It's not! We don't have it yet."

"You're kidding, we don't? When is it going to arrive?" asked Brad.

"It was supposed to be here yesterday. I checked the web site last night and learned it was shipped yesterday. My guess is that it could be as late as Tuesday or Wednesday before it arrives," said John. "It's going to be another rough weekend. Brad, you are going to be here this weekend, aren't you? I assume you don't have another weekend trip planned."

"You're so funny," responded Brad. "Yes, I'm going to be here." Changing the subject, he asked, "How is the temporary fix to the web site working?"

"We're getting by. I cut out several of our web site modules," explained John. "We are, however, receiving a significant amount of email and phone messages asking about the status of the features we've eliminated. We are responding with a message that the features are temporarily down due to high demand and that we are upgrading to a new server to correct the problem."

"I guess there isn't much else we can do until we get the new server," said Brad.

"There is something else we need to mention to you," noted Courtney. "Did we tell you about Will's car accident?"

"Of course you did," responded Brad quickly.

"Well, it's been so crazy around here, I couldn't remember if we talked about that," answered Courtney. "On Thursday, John got a call from Will's attorney explaining that the person in the other car was injured and is seeking compensation. The attorney indicated that, in the end, *MoviesDoorToDoor.com* may be held accountable."

"You're kidding?" responded Brad. "What does our company have to do Will's accident?"

"The attorney believes we're responsible for the damages, since Will's accident occurred while he was on company business," explained Courtney. "We have since learned from Garrett, our attorney, that Will doesn't have car insurance."

"What makes it worse is that we apparently neglected to obtain the appropriate kind of insurance to cover damages incurred by employees while acting as agents of our company," said John.

"You guys are the bearer of bad news today. Don't you have anything good to tell me?" asked Brad. "What does all this mean? Does Garrett think the other party has a real case against us?"

"He's researching it now," noted Courtney. "But, his initial reaction is that it would be best to settle this out of court."

"How much are we liable for?" asked Brad.

"Well, we don't know yet," answered Courtney. "As a matter of fact, we haven't officially received notice of a claim."

The three talked for a while longer. They decided there wasn't much they could do until they got more information from the attorney.

John went to the back office to work, while Brad and Courtney organized movies in the display area. As they started placing new movies on the shelves, Courtney said, "Brad, I hope I'm not intruding. But, I consider us to be very close friends. What's the deal with your trip last weekend? Who's this woman traveling with you?"

"Her name is Maggie," volunteered Brad. "She works at our client in Austin."

"Is there more to it than just that?" asked Courtney.

After a short pause, Brad responded hesitantly, "Maybe you can help me figure out the answer because I'm not sure. I could use a female's perspective."

"Okay, I'm listening," noted Courtney.

Brad told Courtney about all the time he had been spending with Maggie. His description of the past weekend made it clear to Courtney that he had fallen for Maggie. Courtney found it interesting to see how much Brad was struggling to let his feelings be known. It was also obvious that Maggie had similar feelings, but Brad was having a difficult time believing it. She couldn't believe Brad left Austin without disclosing his true feelings to Maggie.

After talking for quite a while, Courtney finally said, "You need to call her immediately. You can't leave her in the dark. A woman is only going to wait for so long."

"Are you sure I need to call her?" asked Brad.

"Trust me, Brad," answered Courtney quickly. "You'll be sorry if you don't."

"Okay. But, there is one more thing I need to talk to you about before I call," noted Brad.

"What's that?" asked Courtney.

"I meant to tell you and John about this earlier today. But, given all the latest developments here, I didn't get to it," said Brad. After a brief pause, he said, "The client in Austin has offered me a full-time job with a strong financial package."

"You're kidding me, right?" asked Courtney.

"Not this time," responded Brad. "This looks like an incredible opportunity, even if Maggie wasn't there. When you add Maggie to the picture, the offer is even more enticing. This would give Maggie and me a chance to really get to know each other better."

"You need to separate the job offer from your personal life," advised Courtney. "You shouldn't take the job just to be with Maggie. If the relationship is meant to be, you can make it work even without taking the job in Austin."

"The real dilemma is that the job would be great," noted Brad.

"Yeah, but what about your ties to *MoviesDoorToDoor.com*?" asked Courtney. "One of the reasons we created this business is to get out of the corporate world and be our own boss. I think Maggie is really clouding the picture."

"I know what you're saying," responded Brad. "I'm totally confused and don't know what I'm going to do. I must admit that the big reason I enjoyed going to Austin was because of Maggie." After a pause, he said, "I guess the first thing I need to do is call Maggie."

At just that moment, a UPS delivery person walked into the store noting he had a large shipment for drop off. Courtney immediately responded, "That's great. I bet it's our new server." She yelled for John to come out front.

John passed Brad on his way out from the back of the store and commented, "Hey, Brad, where are you going? I need your help unpacking the server."

"Hold on, John. I need to make a phone call first," responded Brad abruptly.

"What phone call could be that important?" asked John.

Courtney jumped in quickly, "John, let him go. I'll explain later."

"Whatever!" muttered John. But, he yelled to Brad, "Make it short, Brad!"

Brad was glad to catch Maggie on the phone at her apartment. But, his nervousness quickly consumed him, and he could barely speak.

"Hello," answered Maggie.

"Hey, Maggie. It's Brad."

"Hey!" responded Maggie excitedly. "I wasn't expecting to hear from you so soon. But, I'm glad you called. What's up?"

Brad didn't know how to begin. So, he said, "I just wanted to let you know I made it back safely to Raleigh."

"Oh, that's great," responded Maggie in a puzzled fashion. Trying to think of something to say, she added, "I hope the trip was uneventful."

"Yeah, it was fine," responded Brad. After an awkward pause, he went on to say, "I've been thinking back to how much fun we had last weekend at your parent's lake house and wish we could be there again this weekend."

"I had a great time, too," responded Maggie.

"I'm realizing that I left Austin yesterday not knowing where you and I might be going, if anywhere," noted Brad.

"What do you mean?" asked Maggie.

"Well, I'm finding that I have you on my mind all the time and wanted to know if you have similar feelings." He finally blurted, "I want us to be more than friends."

Maggie's heart was racing as she quickly responded, "Why didn't you say this in the car yesterday? I kept waiting for you to bring this up on our way to the airport."

"I couldn't get the nerve to bring it up," answered Brad. "I'm not good at taking rejection."

"Well, I'm glad you got the nerve to call me today," responded Maggie. "I, too, would like us to be more than friends. You've been on my mind constantly since you left. I was afraid that once you were on the airplane, I might not see you anytime soon."

With a sigh of relief, Brad added, "I'm glad this is out on the table. You can see why I haven't dated that much. I'm not very good at dealing with these kinds of things."

"I'm glad you think that," responded Maggie. "Otherwise, someone else would have grabbed you by now."

"I was wondering if you would be interested in visiting me here in Raleigh," noted Brad. "I would like for us to get to know each other better."

"I'd love to come," responded Maggie. "When should I?"

Brad answered, "Let me check the Internet for available flights. Is there any weekend you can't come?"

"I'm wide open for the next month," answered Maggie.

"That's great," responded Brad. "I'll check flights later today." They talked for quite a while longer before hanging up. Afterwards, Brad walked back into the store area with a huge smile on his face.

"Looks like your phone conversation went well," commented Courtney.

"You've been on the phone this whole time?" asked John abruptly. "I thought you were going to make it short!"

"Oh, John. Can't you see he's in love?" asked Courtney. Brad immediately turned red.

"In love?" laughed John. "How could one phone call cause that?"

"John, you're clueless," noted Courtney.

Changing the subject, Brad asked, "Where's the new server?"

John was so excited to have the server, he shifted his focus to that. Courtney thought to herself, "John sure loves his techie toys. He could go on a one-person mission to the moon as long as he had enough gadgets to entertain him along the way."

* * * * *

Brad and John worked through the next day wiring the server and re-installing all the web site features John had temporarily disabled. While they were working, Brad asked John, "Did we ever figure out what actually caused our server to crash?"

"Obviously, the number of hits to our web site has increased dramatically," responded John. "During the weekend it crashed, our volume of hits was the highest ever."

"If we are getting that many hits, seems like our rental volumes should be significantly increasing as well," commented Brad.

"I really don't know what's happening," answered John. "It could be that customers all want the same movies. So, we are getting hits to the site, but no orders are being generated once the customers realize the movies they want are already rented and not available."

"That might be the case," noted Brad. "But, the huge increase in hits seems so dramatic compared to our actual rental volumes. It's hard to believe they can't be finding other movies they might want to rent. This is especially puzzling since our web site search engine generates alternative movie selections based on the movies they are trying to rent. Surely there are other acceptable movie alternatives for them."

"I'd have to admit, it's a puzzle to me as well," said John. "At one point, we talked about modifying the web site to capture better information on customer utilization of the web site. Unfortunately, that was put on the back burner because of other more critical modifications we wanted to make to the web site. The result is that we don't have enough good information now to answer these questions."

"Are you sure?" asked Brad. "We do require customers to give us their name when using our web site."

"That's not totally correct," answered John. "They only give us their name once they decide to rent a movie. That adds them to our database of registered users, which we use to get the delivery address."

"Could we change the registration process to require customers to give us their name as soon as they access the web site?" asked Brad. "That way we could figure out who's accessing the site without renting movies from us."

"That could be done," answered John. "It would require all new customers to completely register during their first visit on the site before proceeding further."

"Given our growing customer base, I don't think we need to worry about whether this new feature would turn off new customers," noted Brad. "And, this would allow us to have better information about who's accessing the web site."

"I can work on fixing that tomorrow night, after I get done at Interconnectivity," said John.

Brad asked, "Should we fill Courtney in on what we're thinking before we do that?"

"Probably so," noted John. "I'll mention it to her tonight."

* * * * *

Maggie was excited that she could visit Brad in Raleigh just two weeks after he left Austin. She definitely felt the relationship was moving in a positive direction.

On Friday night when she was scheduled to arrive, Courtney teased Brad, "You're dressed better than usual tonight! Are those new clothes? I'll have to make sure Maggie knows this isn't how you normally dress."

Brad quickly responded, "You're beginning to sound like John. You must be hanging around him too much."

"What are you planning to do tonight after she arrives?" asked Courtney.

"First, I thought we would drop by the store to show her what it looks like," responded Brad. "Then, I thought we'd grab dinner at a nice restaurant."

"Don't come by here," responded Courtney. "Seeing our store isn't why she's coming to Raleigh. Wait until tomorrow to show her *MoviesDoorTo-Door.com*. Go enjoy a meal with her tonight. I look forward to meeting her when you drop her off at my apartment for the night. I'm glad she's willing to stay with me."

"I guess you're right," noted Brad. "Any more advice?"

"You don't need my advice," responded Courtney. "You've managed to catch Maggie's attention all by yourself. I haven't helped at all so far."

Brad was a little anxious by the time Maggie's plane arrived. The flight was over an hour late. He hoped she wouldn't be too tired to enjoy a nice, relaxing dinner.

As it turned out, they were both so excited to be together that they were full of energy. Dinner was great. Brad hated to end the conversation after midnight, but felt like he needed to get Maggie to Courtney's apartment before it was too late.

When he dropped Maggie off at Courtney's apartment, the three of them visited for a little while. It was great to see how well Courtney and Maggie hit it off. Just before Brad left, they agreed he would come by around 10:00 a.m. the next day.

Brad arrived early the next day with bagels and coffee in hand. He just couldn't control his desire to see Maggie again. Courtney and Maggie had been up for a while enjoying each other's company. Courtney was beginning to feel like they were soul mates, since they appeared to have so much in common. When Maggie went to the bedroom to get her purse, Courtney whispered to Brad, "I'm impressed! She's wonderful."

"Do you really think so?" asked Brad.

"Oh gosh, definitely!" said Courtney emphatically. "Make sure that today is special."

"I was planning on taking her to the Botanical Gardens for a picnic," said Brad.

"That's perfect," responded Courtney.

The rest of the weekend flew by. When Brad and Maggie were back at the airport on Sunday night, he kept thinking, "How could the weekend already be over?" They agreed he would visit her in Austin in three weeks, which seemed like a long time for both of them. But, that's the best they could do for now. At least they would be able to talk on the phone each day.

* * * * *

Feedback from customers over the next couple of weeks was positive. They were glad to have all the advanced web site features restored. And, they liked the quicker response time. The new server was making a huge difference.

Work was so hectic at both Interconnectivity and *MoviesDoorToDoor.com* that none of them had a chance to analyze the new information collected from the new customer registration process.

Brad, Courtney, and John decided to order pizza one Wednesday night to go over the new information collected over the last few weeks. When they met, Brad commented, "Boy, this brings back memories of our first days of starting the business. Remember all those late-night pizzas we ordered?" Courtney and John agreed.

They all huddled around a computer terminal in the back room to start looking over the information already captured. John pulled up the database of registered users and was shocked when he realized there were over 50,000 registered users in the database.

They all sat stunned. Finally, Courtney asked, "How could that be true? We don't deliver to that many people. Something is wrong."

"Let's look at some of the users in the database. Maybe we have multiple users included per family," said Brad.

They spent some time scanning the database, which was organized alphabetically. Surprisingly, they found very few duplicate names. Courtney then said, "Let's sort this database by zip code to see which areas are most prevalent."

"Good idea," noted John. "I'll do that now."

Several of the zip codes were unrecognizable. A large number of zip codes represented areas outside of North Carolina. As they looked closer at some of the addresses, they discovered a number of web site users who lived on the west coast, including Alaska and Hawaii. It looked like they had a registered user in every state in the U.S. And, a number of them appeared to be outside the U.S.

"This is unbelievable," commented Brad. "I had no idea that many people are using our web site. No wonder our server crashed."

"I wish we had this information before we purchased the new server," whined John. "We could have programmed our web site to restrict its use to people in our delivery area. That would have cut down on the web site traffic, allowing us to continue using our old server, which is now sitting in the corner."

"John, wait a second," responded Courtney. "This is fantastic news. We have a huge new market to tap into."

"What do you mean?" asked John. "It would take a tremendous amount of effort and resources to develop a network of store locations around the country. There's no way we could do that on our own."

"No, that's not what I'm thinking about," commented Courtney. "We could market our web site to other video stores around the country and charge a fee to those stores. We could set up something like the FTD service florists use."

Brad jumped in saying, "Wait, I have an even better idea. It appears that people are accessing our web site to help them pick movies they would like to watch. We could charge a subscription fee to users of our site. Just think, if we charge $1 a month, we would generate an additional $50,000 monthly from our current customer database."

"Whoa, slow down a minute. That sounds too unbelievable," responded John.

"Right now, we are providing a free service to people all around the world by helping them select movies using our search engine," explained Brad. "We might as well charge for that service. I bet most people would be willing to pay a dollar. If I think a service is valuable, I'm willing to pay especially if we're talking such a small amount. A cup of coffee is cheaper! A lot of people do that every day!"

"What about the local users who actually order movies for delivery. Might this chase them away?" asked Courtney.

"I don't think so," responded Brad. "But, we could waive the fee if a user rents at least one movie during that month."

"That sounds reasonable," noted Courtney.

"If this really works, we could get out of the movie delivery business," added John. "We could focus all our efforts on the search engine. That's what we do best, anyway."

"I don't know about that," commented Brad. "Given the downturn in Internet-only businesses, we may want to maintain and expand our 'brick and mortar' presence. The good news is, that if this really works, we would have enough resources to start on that expansion."

"If we start charging for access to our movie selection search engine, we're going to have to make several changes to our web site features," noted Courtney.

"You're right," commented John. "The major change would involve the use of a user i.d. and password before customers could access the system. This would ensure that only paying customers can access the system. Since we already require our web site users to register when they log onto our system the first time, it won't require much additional work to re-program our system to capture the credit card payment information for the subscription fee."

"Is it possible that the subscription fee will turn away potential customers?" asked Courtney. "I think customers would want to see how the search engine works before deciding whether they want to pay a fee for this service."

"That's a good point," noted Brad. "What if we program the web site so that a new customer gets five free uses of the web site movie search engine before they are requested to subscribe to the service. That would give them five different chances to work with the search engine before paying for it."

"Sounds good," noted John.

"Don't forget that we also have to incorporate a mechanism to waive the fee when the customer rents a movie," added Courtney.

"Let me grab a piece of paper to make some notes of what we're saying," noted John. He found a few scrap sheets of paper and jotted down their thoughts.

After they reviewed some of the items they had discussed, John said, "I think I ought to be able to program these features into our web site in about a week."

"We may want to have a slow transition into this," noted Brad. "Seems like we need to warn our customers that we're moving towards a subscription-based service. Perhaps, we could post a message on the opening page of the web site noting that the search engine access will convert to a subscription-based service starting next month."

"Do we need to tell them the reason why we are switching?" asked Courtney.

John responded, "We could explain that demand for the web search engine has increased substantially over the last several months. In order to properly support the web site and ensure availability of the service for customers ordering movie deliveries, we will be charging a nominal $1 fee for non-movie renting customers. Hopefully most customers will understand the need to charge for the services they use and will find the small fee reasonable."

Brad noted, "Now that I've thought about this for a minute, I am a little concerned that charging them $1 on a monthly basis is going to make the processing for us too time consuming. Why don't we charge customers $12 for access to the search engine database for a full year? That way we only have to process the access fee once a year rather than once a month."

"That's a good point," noted John. "But, that means we would be charging everyone a subscription fee regardless of whether they rent a movie."

"I'm tired of thinking about all this. It's giving me a headache!" noted Courtney.

"Hey, wait a minute. I have an idea of how we could deal with waiving the fee for customers who rent movies from us," noted Brad.

"Tell us!" responded Courtney.

"We could give the customer a $1 discount for each of the first 12 movies they rent in a year," explained Brad. "That way, they basically end up not having to pay a subscription fee as long as they rent at least 12 movies in a single year."

"I like that idea," commented John. "That won't be too difficult to program. I want to start on this immediately. I don't want to leave money on the table. Too bad we didn't think about this earlier."

Courtney responded, "Well, we had to work on building our customer base first. We couldn't start charging for the movie search engine until customers found it beneficial. And, remember our web site didn't start with all the features it has now."

"Finally, I feel like our dreams for this business are coming true," responded John.

"This is bringing back some of those feelings we had when we first opened our store," commented Brad. "I'm so pumped!"

"Before we leave, let's make sure we're all in agreement," noted John. "I'm going to program the web site so that we charge an annual subscription fee of $12 for use of the movie search engine," explained John. "I'll also include the waiver of the fee for those renting 12 or more movies during the year and I'll set it up so that new customers have five free trials before the subscription fee is charged."

"I think that's what we're all saying," responded Courtney.

Brad agreed and then added, "If this really works, we could have almost $600,000 in the bank by the end the first month we begin charging for the service."

"That's unbelievable," commented John.

* * * * *

Later that week, Brad received a call from Cara who was following up on her earlier job proposal. Brad apologized that he hadn't been able to make a final decision about her offer, but committed to responding in the next couple of days.

As soon as he got off the phone with Cara, he decided he better call Maggie. To this point, Brad hadn't talked to Maggie about the offer because he felt that might put too much pressure on both of them. But, now he felt like it couldn't be postponed any longer.

When they finally talked, Brad told Maggie about the job offer and he also updated her on the latest developments at *MoviesDoorToDoor.com*. In some ways he was relieved when Maggie suggested that he not take the offer. She felt that the potential at *MoviesDoorToDoor.com* was too great for him to leave Raleigh right now. In other ways, he wished she had encouraged him to take the job so that they could spend more time together. But as they talked about the opportunity, she helped Brad think through all the important issues. And she made it very clear, that their relationship was not contingent on his decision. It was incredible to see how supportive she was.

A little bit later, Brad called Cara to tell her he wouldn't be able to accept her offer. He explained that there were commitments in Raleigh that he just couldn't walk away from right now. Cara understood his reasons and noted that she would like to keep in touch with him in case the situation changed. Brad felt good about their conversation.

When Brad later shared his decision with Courtney and John, they were both relieved. Courtney knew it was a tough decision because of his feelings for Maggie. John, on the other hand thought Brad was totally crazy even considering the offer. He couldn't imagine Brad leaving *MoviesDoorTo-Door.com* right now. Things were looking too good for Brad to jeopardize them just for Maggie. When John mentioned his thoughts to Courtney, she was amazed at his lack of sensitivity.

Discussion Questions

1.   *MoviesDoorToDoor.com* financed the purchase of a new server with debt. What journal entry would be made to record the acquisition?

2.   What effect would the purchase of the new server have on working capital and the current ratio?

3.   Would the new server be reflected on the financial statements as a short-term asset or a long-term asset?

4.   How would the financial statements reflect the use of that server over time?

5.   How would *MoviesDoorToDoor.com* record the collection of subscription fees? Will those fees be shown immediately as revenue at the point of collection?

6.   How would they account for the waiver of the subscription fee when the first 12 movies are rented in a given year?

7.   *MoviesDoorToDoor.com* will have to pay income taxes on the subscription fees in the year of collection, even though some of those subscription fees won't be earned until the next year. How should the income taxes paid on the subscription fees be reflected in the financial statements? Support your answer.

8. Assume *MoviesDoorToDoor.com* actually does collect $600,000 in subscription fees. What would investors think if company management kept all the cash in a checking account at the bank?

9. How will the following financial statement ratios be affected by the collection of the subscription fees?
   a. Current ratio
   b. Return on equity
   c. Earnings per share
   d. Debt to equity

10. Assume the subscription fees are collected. Describe the pros and cons of paying off the loans to the bank and Courtney's parents early.

Chapter 11
The Negotiations Begin

Brad, Courtney, and John were a little disappointed when they went live with the subscription fee. Only 30,000 registered database users initially continued as subscribers. Their disappointment didn't last long once they focused on the fact they still grossed $360,000 in just one month. And, they were convinced there were plenty of new customers who could be enticed to join.

To increase the visibility of their movie search engine, they moved to Internet advertising on the web sites of various search engines. They felt that this move would help make more people aware of their web site. They also began advertising the movie search engine in some of the more popular entertainment-related magazines.

Another decision they made was to significantly expand the searchable database to include movies not carried at the store. Brad and Courtney were particularly convinced that the demand for the movie search engine would increase if the number of movies covered in the database was more inclusive. They also expanded the number of movies included in inventory at the store so that their local customers would have more selections.

Opening new stores was also a consideration; however, Brad, Courtney and John decided that it was first critical to train reliable managers to run new stores. As a starter, they hired a full-time manager to work with them at the current location to learn the business. It was their hope that the manager could eventually run a new location, which under their current plan would open every six months.

With the security of having $360,000 in the bank, Brad, Courtney, and John decided they could tender their resignations at Interconnectivity. It was tough to surrender the security of having a stable job, but they felt *MoviesDoorTo-Door.com* wouldn't be able to expand sufficiently without their full-time attention.

Now that they were full-time employees, they agreed to give themselves an annual salary of $60,000 each. They also arranged for health insurance and other benefits for them and the new manager who was receiving a salary of $40,000. They estimated their total annual payroll related costs including fringe benefits to be about $260,000 for the four of them. While that took a big chunk of their $360,000 subscription fees, they believed the opportunities for future growth would be realized much more quickly if they could concentrate on the business full time. They also felt there would likely be a high rate of subscription renewals on an annual basis for quite a while.

The only major negative event occurring during this same time period was the settlement of the lawsuit related to Will's car accident. Their attorney advised that it would be cheaper to settle the case to avoid defending themselves in court. As a result, they reluctantly signed a check for $40,000 as settlement. Soon after that, they worked with their insurance agent to be certain the business had more than adequate liability coverage for these types of events.

Brad and Courtney focused most of their efforts over the next six months expanding the searchable database. Because most of the customers subscribing to the movie selection search engine service weren't renting movies for delivery from *MoviesDoorToDoor.com*, inclusion of movies in the database that they did not carry in the store didn't create major customer-relation problems. Fortunately, all their efforts were apparently paying off, since the total paying subscribers quickly built back to 50,000 in just six months after launching the new subscription-based service. And, they felt confident that there was still a huge untapped market.

Brad and Courtney viewed a ton of movies to obtain information to include in the movie descriptions and classification criteria needed for the database. Brad's liberal arts degree, along with their interests in reading books, was a big help in expanding the database. Brad loved sharing that news with his dad, who continued to tease him about his college education.

John continued to maintain the server, given his fascination with technology. He was constantly upgrading the server software, and continued to find ways to improve the operating efficiency and security of the system. He was consistently seen in the back room working with the computer.

For the first time in quite a while, all three of them felt like their lives were back under control. Unfortunately, John wasn't using his extra time to be with Courtney, which continued to frustrate her. He was filling his new free time with running and with his rekindled interest in weight lifting. John spent most of his time at *MoviesDoorToDoor.com*, training for a new road race, or at the gym. As a result, Brad was back to mediating between Courtney and John.

Brad was really going through his personal funds flying to Austin on a regular basis to see Maggie. At least he was building up tons of frequent flyer mileage. It seemed like every weekend either Brad or Maggie was usually traveling so they could be together. Their relationship was now to the point where Maggie was thinking about moving to Raleigh. But, two things were holding her back. First, she was reluctant to give up her job in Austin. Second, she was concerned about moving so far away from her family in Texas. The two of them agreed that she should stay put for a little while longer.

Courtney was becoming envious of Brad and Maggie's relationship. She felt like Brad and Maggie spent more quality time together than she did with John, which was beginning to bug her. Courtney knew that if she mentioned her frustrations to John, her words would go in one of John's ears and out the other. She longed for the early days in their relationship when John actively pursued her. How ironic that their roles in the relationship had reversed.

One day while Courtney was working in the back of the store, a customer came in asking for her. The store manager, Kate, stepped to the back of the store and said, "Hey, Courtney there's a great-looking guy out here asking for you. I've never seen him before."

"I wonder who that could be," muttered Courtney.

When Courtney walked into the store, she suddenly screamed once she realized who it was. Thinking someone was hurt, everyone else in the store stopped when they heard her voice.

"Steve, is that you?" asked Courtney.

"Yep," responded Steve.

Courtney started to run to hug him, but then the memory of how he dumped her flashed across her mind. They hadn't seen each other in almost three years and her emotions started to overwhelm her.

"I started to call you before I dropped by," explained Steve. "But, I wasn't sure you would take my call. So, I decided to come see you."

"How did you know where I was?" asked Courtney.

"I've been checking your web site ever since you went live with it," noted Steve. "As a matter of fact, I'm one of your paying subscribers. You know how much I like watching movies. I'll have to admit, you've done a fantastic job developing your search engine."

Customers in the store went back to looking at movies on the shelves. Kate appeared to be busy at the front desk, but her curiosity was killing her. She listened as she shuffled things on the counter.

Courtney then asked Steve, "What are you doing in Raleigh?"

"With the downturn in the technology sector of the economy, my job in the Silicon Valley got eliminated," explained Steve. "I found a good opportunity back here in Raleigh with a large telecommunications company. As it turns out, it's a good time for me to be home. Just before I lost my job, I learned that my mom has cancer. So, I decided I needed to be closer to my family as well."

"I'm sorry to hear about your mom," responded Courtney. "How is she doing?"

"She's a fighter," noted Steve. "We're just taking one day at a time."

While they were talking, John walked into the store with sandwiches for lunch. Courtney was speechless when she realized it was John. John called to her, "Courtney, I have your sandwich. I'll meet you in the back."

"Hey, John come over here. I've got someone for you to meet," said Courtney hesitantly. "While I don't think you've met face-to-face, I know you've talked on the phone. Do you remember my friend, Steve?"

John was silent. Finally, he said, "Oh yeah, Steve. Nice to meet you. What brings you to town?"

"I've actually moved back to the area," responded Steve.

"Why don't you join us for a sandwich?" offered John.

"Oh no, I don't want to intrude," answered Steve. "Courtney, would you mind if I called you later?"

"No," said Courtney. "Let me give you my telephone number."

"That's great," said Steve. "I look forward to catching up with you. I better go."

Once Steve was gone, John said, "Wow, that's a surprise."

"You're telling me," responded Courtney.

* * * * *

Later that week, Courtney met Steve for lunch. While she was a little apprehensive about seeing him, they ended up having an enjoyable time catching up with one another. She recalled the good qualities that originally attracted her to him. His wit and ability to give his undivided attention resonated with her. He seemed like the old Steve she knew in college. Her negative feelings about how they ended their relationship were diminishing.

Courtney surprised herself when she let Steve talk her into meeting him for dinner in a couple of weeks. The more she thought about it, she began to wonder how John would react. Based on John's apparent lack of interest in what was going on with Steve, she decided it wasn't worth mentioning.

John's main focus at this point in time was following *MoviesDoorTo-Door.com's* increased visibility on major search engines. He couldn't stop searching movie related topics on major search engines to see where *MoviesDoorToDoor.com's* web site appeared in the results generated. He was encouraged to find that their web site was rising on the search results.

When Courtney returned from lunch, she found John working on the computer. "John, I can't believe you're searching the Internet again. Don't you have anything else better to do?"

"You're not going to believe this," responded John. "Our web site has hit the top ten. I just entered the term 'movie reviews' and our web site was the tenth one listed in the search results. I get similar results when I use other terms, such as 'movie rentals' or 'videos'. This is going to give our web site so much visibility. I can see our subscription revenues really growing. This is unbelievable."

"That's great," responded Courtney. "Apparently our Internet advertising is paying off. Brad will be excited to hear this news, too."

"We might have another great opportunity to generate additional revenues," noted John.

"How's that?" asked Courtney.

"Now that our web site is more visible, other companies may be interested in advertising on our web site," explained John. "We might be able to sell some banner advertising space on our web site. For example, movie producers may be interested in advertising new movies coming out in theatres. And, they may want to feature recent movies about to be released in video and DVD formats."

"Who's going to market that to movie producers?" asked Courtney.

"Hey, we can figure that out," responded John. "Let's not let that be a reason for our not doing it. Maybe our ad agency can help us."

"John, aren't we making enough money now?" asked Courtney. "When will you ever lighten up and give us some personal time. You're working harder at *MoviesDoorToDoor.com* than when you held two jobs."

"I'd rather work hard now, so that I can have more personal time later," responded John. "You've got to grab opportunities when they present themselves. We can't wait."

"Yeah, but at some point you've got to stop deferring the fun parts of life," noted Courtney. "You can't keep putting your personal life on hold."

"Come on, Courtney. You're beginning to sound like you're not enjoying life," said John. "I'm still enjoying this wild ride."

"My life is exciting," responded Courtney defensively. "However, I don't want business to consume all my waking moments."

Just then, Brad walked in. Courtney quickly said, "Brad, would you talk some sense into John. He's going to work himself to the grave, if he's not careful."

"Don't drag me into your arguments," teased Brad.

"Oh, we're not arguing," responded Courtney.

"Yeah, I'm just being nagged by Courtney," noted John.

"Thanks," said Courtney sarcastically to John.

"Hey, Brad. Guess what we just figured out?" said John.

"What's that?" asked Brad.

"Our web site is starting to hit the top ten on web search engines," explained John. "This ought to really boost our subscription revenues due to the increased visibility. Your idea to go to the subscription service was brilliant."

"That's awesome," noted Brad.

Courtney and John updated Brad about their discussion of the banner advertising ideas. Brad thought it was worth pursuing. As a first step, they decided to contact their ad agency to get started.

* * * * *

The next few months proved to be crazy. The number of subscribers continued to increase. And, the implementation of banner ads on *MoviesDoorToDoor.com's* web site was also paying off. Business was great.

Then, the most shocking event occurred. They were approached by a national movie rental chain that was interested in discussing a potential buyout of their business. Apparently, senior management of the national chain was quite aware of *MoviesDoorToDoor.com's* web site. It was clear that management of the chain had done their homework. They indicated that *MoviesDoorToDoor.com's* web site would compliment rentals at all the national chain's store locations. And, the web site would provide a strategic advantage when movie rentals moved to digital downloading via the Internet.

Brad, Courtney and John were blown away by the initial proposal. This possibility wasn't on their radar screen at all. Up to this point, their strategic planning was focused on expanding the searchable movie database and opening additional stores. The three of them were working towards eventually relinquishing more of the day-to-day responsibilities to professional managers like Kate. Being the target of an acquisition introduced a totally new perspective on their futures.

Brad and Courtney were instantly ready to sell. They saw this as an opportunity to move on with their personal goals. They believed the potential pay-out to each of them would keep them from worrying about working ever again. It was as if they were winning the lottery.

On the other hand, John wasn't sure he was ready to give up control of the company. It was his baby, and he couldn't envision letting it go. He believed that the company had just scraped the surface of the market and wanted to be involved with the company through this growth period. More importantly, John wasn't sure what he would do with himself if he didn't have his job at *MoviesDoorToDoor.com*. The company had become a major part of his life. And, in his view, the best was yet to come.

After discussing the potential acquisition over with Brad and Courtney for quite a while, John began to realize that it was going to be difficult to change their minds. At least he was able to convince them to proceed cautiously so they could strengthen their negotiating position. All three agreed to seek advice from several people, including Brad's dad, Rebecca, and their attorney.

At this point, the information from the national chain was lacking specific details of the transaction. While the ballpark range of the purchase price being discussed seemed very good, Brad, Courtney and John knew that *MoviesDoorToDoor.com* had so much untapped potential that they needed time to digest and analyze the pros and cons of such an offer.

Senior management of the national chain indicated that they could provide more specifics on the offer once they obtained and analyzed financial and operating information from *MoviesDoorToDoor.com*. Specifically, they would need to receive audited financial statements from *MoviesDoorToDoor.com* for the three years since its inception.

That request took Brad, Courtney, and John by surprise. They had never engaged a CPA firm to audit their financial statements, since there hadn't been an overwhelming need. Their current investors didn't expect them to be audited, and the bank hadn't made that a loan condition. None of them had a good understanding of what was involved with obtaining audited financial statements.

Senior management of the chain made it clear that the negotiations couldn't proceed further until *MoviesDoorToDoor.com* was willing to have their financial statements audited. These reports would help establish the final purchase price offer. Too much money was going to be at stake to proceed without having assurances on the credibility of the underlying financial reports.

They suggested that Brad, Courtney, and John allow the national chain's external auditor to perform the required audit work with the audit fees being paid by the chain. John was uncomfortable having the chain's auditor perform the work, as he was not sure their external auditor would look out for *MoviesDoorToDoor.com's* best interests. After some discussion, both parties agreed that Brad, Courtney and John could be involved in the selection of a different external auditing firm.

* * * * *

Over the next few days, Brad, Courtney and John talked with several people about the potential buyout. The reaction from everyone was overwhelmingly positive. Everyone recommended that they continue negotiations with the chain to work towards a potential buyout. Most believed there was little downside risk to further discussion.

During the next month, they were able to select and hire the external audit firm. Representatives from the firm met with Brad, Courtney, and John to learn more about the *MoviesDoorToDoor.com* business and to gain an understanding of their accounting systems and records. Fortunately, the auditors were able to assemble a team quickly to get the audit underway. Everyone knew it would be a little messy, given the financial statements had never been prepared by a CPA.

John spent quite a bit of time discussing the potential buyout with his mom. During one of their conversations, a new issue came to light. She wanted to know if Brad, Courtney, and John planned on issuing additional stock to themselves as compensation for all their work in the business. Because none of the three founders received any compensation for their efforts during the first two years of the business, she felt it was reasonable to grant them additional shares of stock in the business as a reward for their hard work. She kept referring to this as their "sweat equity." His mom explained that most public corporations use stock as a primary mechanism to compensate senior officers. She encouraged John to consider issuing additional shares to ensure the three founders were fairly compensated for all their efforts in building the business to its current position.

John quickly realized that his mom was making a great point. They had all worked so hard over the first couple of years juggling duties at Interconnectivity and *MoviesDoorToDoor.com*. He agreed that it was important to be compensated appropriately for those efforts.

When John first approached Brad and Courtney, they both seemed to be in agreement that they should pursue this issue. John believed that the total compensation for all three of them should be about $300,000. He argued that $300,000 would be approximately equal to the total compensation they would have paid to professional managers to handle all of what they did during the initial startup years. Brad and Courtney seemed to think his suggested amount was reasonable.

John also indicated that using the $5 per share price they used to determine the initial stock allocation to investors at the beginning of the business would still be reasonable. That meant they would allocate an additional 60,000 shares of stock among the three of them. He suggested they take a night to think about the allocation before discussing it further the next day.

Brad decided to call his dad to run the idea by him. While his dad agreed they deserved to be compensated for their efforts, he pointed out that Brad's ownership interests would be diluted if they decided to allocate the 60,000 shares evenly among the three of them. His dad reminded Brad that based on the initial issuance of stock when the business was started, Brad held 7,200 of the 18,000 shares outstanding, giving him a 40 percent interest in the business. If the three decided to issue an additional 60,000 shares of stock as compensation for their work, Brad would end up holding 27,200 of the 78,000 total shares outstanding after the issuance. That would lower his percentage ownership to approximately 35 percent.

27,200 shares / 78,000 shares outstanding = 34.9 percentage ownership

That meant Brad would receive less in the eventual buyout if they decided to allocate the additional shares, since he would be holding 35 percent of the shares to be purchased by the national chain. On the other hand, if they left everything as is, he would be holding 40 percent of the shares to be purchased.

His dad also pointed out that Courtney and John's ownership interests would increase, if they issued the additional 60,000 shares. Courtney and John each currently had 3,600 of the 18,000 shares outstanding, which represented a 20 percent ownership stake for them individually. If they issued the additional 60,000 shares, Courtney and John's individual ownership amounts would increase to 23,600 shares out of 78,000 shares outstanding giving each of them a 30.3% ownership stake in the business.

23,600 shares / 78,000 shares = 30.3 percentage ownership

After Brad and his dad talked for quite a while, Brad concluded that while he would receive less from the buyout, he believed issuing the additional shares was the appropriate thing to do. They had all put in a lot of effort in those first two years. And, the compensation amount being considered seemed reasonable.

* * * * *

The next morning, Brad walked into *MoviesDoorToDoor.com* with a big smile on his face. He was growing happier each day as he considered the potential buyout that seemed to be developing.

When John saw Brad, he said, "Finally, you're here. Courtney and I have been waiting for you."

"Oh, I didn't realize we were planning to meet first thing today," responded Brad.

John quickly responded, "We weren't. But, Courtney and I are curious to hear your thoughts about allocating the 60,000 shares among the three of us."

"After talking with my dad and thinking about it for a while, I believe it makes sense for us to issue the additional shares," responded Brad. "I think we've all worked extremely hard and deserve fair compensation for those efforts."

"That's great," responded John. "Sounds like we're all in agreement. Courtney and I have been trying to figure out how much effort each of us has put forth over the first two years of the business. We've concluded that Courtney and I should each receive 23,000 shares with you receiving the balance of 14,000 shares."

Brad sat frozen with a shocked expression on his face. The idea of compensating each of them differently hadn't even crossed his mind. Once he had a chance to catch his breath, he responded, "What do you mean?"

"Well, as we all know you spent a lot of time this past year in Austin and thus haven't been here as much to contribute towards *MoviesDoorToDoor.com*," responded John. "For example, when the server crashed, Courtney and I had to give up our vacation to San Francisco in order to handle that crisis. We took care of everything, including selecting and acquiring the new server and obtaining the financing with the bank. Meanwhile, you were off gallivanting around with Maggie at her lake house."

"While I'll acknowledge that you guys did spend more time working at *MoviesDoorToDoor.com* during that time, we all agreed that I had to take the assignment in Austin," responded Brad. "Recall that before I accepted the Austin assignment, I set up a lunch meeting for us to discuss the dilemma of my being assigned to that engagement. At that time, you both indicated that I had to take the Austin assignment to cover for the three of us. As a result, I don't think it's fair to penalize me when Interconnectivity basically forced me to take on the Austin engagement. Had you been asked to go, I'm confident we would have agreed it was something you had to do for the benefit of all of us. Unfortunately, I'm the one who got the luck of the draw for that assignment. Remember, we were under pressure to carry our fair load at Interconnectivity. We had no choice but for me to accept the Austin assignment."

"Yeah, but when we made that decision, we thought the Austin engagement would only last a month," noted John. "My guess is that you were dragging it on, given your personal interests in Maggie."

"Don't go there!" said Brad defensively. "There was no way for me to extend that engagement beyond what was required. It just so happens that my team did such a great job, the client decided to significantly expand the engagement. Because Interconnectivity was billing them for our time on an hourly basis, the client was very aware of the expenses of the project and monitored them closely. The client wouldn't have allowed any inappropriate extension of our work there." Brad continued, "It's insulting for you to imply that I would inappropriately bill a client for personal gain."

"Well, you sure didn't try to get off the job," said John.

"You're right," said Brad. "I didn't want to destroy my career, given it was my main livelihood. I had to act rationally." He went on, "If you're going to pursue this unequal distribution of the 60,000 shares, then I'll vote to reject the idea of providing any stock distribution as compensation for our work. We can retain our existing stock positions."

"Your entitled to do that," answered John. "But, I'm confident the distribution of additional shares will occur, since you only own 40 percent of the outstanding shares. If Courtney, my mom, and I vote as a block, then your vote won't matter since on a combined basis we'll have a majority position."

Then Brad turned to Courtney who had remained silent throughout this discussion, "Is that going to be your position?"

"I don't know," responded Courtney. "John is trying to point out the additional stress we incurred while you were gone. When you first started the assignment in Austin, things were really rough around here. We worked so many additional hours to cover your absence. And, when the server crashed everything was compounded. While I realize the crash of the server wasn't your fault, the reality is John and I had to handle that incredible burden without you."

"This is unbelievable," commented Brad. "My dad was right. He kept warning me that I should be concerned about the two of you. I knew John might be this greedy, but I'm most surprised at you, Courtney."

Growing more uncomfortable, Courtney responded, "I don't want to talk about this anymore."

"Before we finish this conversation, let me point out something," said Brad. "My dad suggested that I not go along with the distribution since the issuance of additional shares would actually dilute my percentage ownership from 40 percent to 35 percent. In contrast, the percentage held by each of you would go from 20 percent to 30 percent. Obviously, that means the proceeds I would receive from this potential buyout would be less if we go along with the distribution of the 60,000 shares than if we don't. But, I told my dad that I would go along with the additional distribution, since I believed it was the right thing to do. As a team, we created this company from the very beginning and each deserve to be rewarded equally for the work we've incurred. I didn't want greed to get the best of me. And, in the end I hope you won't let it get the best of you."

"Don't try to put a guilt trip on me," said John.

"I'll say the same for you," responded Brad defensively.

Courtney jumped in, "I can't take this anymore. I'm out of here." She immediately walked out of the store and got in her car. Brad and John stared at each other for a moment before Brad decided to leave as well. John stayed around to work more on the server.

* * * * *

About an hour later, Courtney called John from her cell phone, "John. We need to talk. Is Brad there?"

"No," responded John. "I don't know where he is. He took off right after you left."

"Good," noted Courtney. "I just want to talk with you."

"Okay, go ahead," said John.

"I've been thinking while driving around. I believe we should distribute the 60,000 shares evenly. While I agree that you and I put in more effort than Brad, all three of us agreed that Brad should take the Austin assignment. More importantly, Brad's willingness to let the distribution of more shares dilute his ownership percentage indicates to me that he holds our relationship above his desire for money. I don't feel comfortable penalizing him further."

"Well, you could argue that my mom is going to be penalized, too," responded John. "Her ownership percentage is going to decline as well if we make a stock distribution to the three of us."

After a brief pause, Courtney said, "I really don't want to have a huge discussion on this. I've decided that I'm going to vote with Brad. And, you can't change my mind."

"Courtney, I can't believe you're going to do this," said John. "This is a business decision. Don't let your emotions get involved."

"I want to be able to look Brad in the face and feel good about it," responded Courtney. "But, obviously you don't care – you can be so heartless at times. As far as I'm concerned this is a done deal. If I vote with Brad, we'll have a majority position. So whatever Brad and I decide will stand."

John responded, "Courtney, this has implications for our relationship."

"Only if you make it an issue," responded Courtney. "I can see that our conversation is digressing. I'm hanging up."

John slammed down the phone in frustration. He muttered, "What a wimp. She's letting Brad guilt her into an unfair allocation."

* * * * *

Over the next few days, Brad, Courtney, and John avoided one another. They were all fairly busy trying to take care of their individual responsibilities at *MoviesDoorToDoor.com*. John's responsibilities related to preparing the accounting information for the auditors kept him occupied as they worked towards completion of the audited financial statements. There was minimal interaction with representatives of the national chain as the negotiations related to the potential buyout would have to wait for the completion of the audit.

This gave all three of them some time to step back and think about the recent events. There was so much to digest.

Discussion Questions

1.   *MoviesDoorToDoor.com* began selling banner advertising on their web site. Assume that the purchasers of the banner ads agreed to pay a flat fee for the ability to run a banner ad, which would be billed by *MoviesDoorToDoor.com* on a quarterly basis after the ads ran for three months. At the end of each month during the quarter, how should the financial statements reflect the banner advertising fees not yet collected?

2.   What risks would *MoviesDoorToDoor.com* bear if it agrees to bill purchasers of banner advertising space on their web site after the ads have already run?

3.   How will *MoviesDoorToDoor.com* financial statements be affected if purchasers of banner advertising fail to pay for those services?

4.   Some of the companies purchasing banner advertising space on *MoviesDoorToDoor.com's* web site may want to structure payment for those ads to be contingent on the number of times viewers on *MoviesDoorToDoor.com's* web site actually drill down to the advertising purchasers' web sites. What kinds of controls would be needed to bill correctly for those ads?

5.   Brad, Courtney, and John failed to provide any compensation to themselves during the first two years of their business. With hindsight, what kinds of procedures could they have implemented from the start to be able to later compensate each of them fairly?

6.   Describe the nature of the assurance the external auditors will be able to provide about *MoviesDoorToDoor.com's* financial statements once they complete the audit.

7.   Describe differences between a CPA firm's "review" of financial statements and an "audit" of financial statements.

8.   Why would shareholders of a company encourage the compensation of senior management through the issuance of company stock rather than compensate them solely through a fixed salary?

9.   How would the issuance of the additional 60,000 shares affect *MoviesDoorToDoor.com's* earnings per share (EPS) calculation?

10.   Show your calculation of how the distribution of the 60,000 shares to Brad, Courtney, and John would affect John's mom's ownership percentage.

11.   Assume that *MoviesDoorToDoor.com* decides to issue a stock dividend to all stockholders. How would that affect the company's Balance Sheet?

12.   How would recording the advertising revenues when they are earned but before they are collected affect these financial statement ratios?
   a.   Current ratio
   b.   Return on equity
   c.   Earnings per share
   d.   Debt to equity

Chapter 12
What Next?

The auditors were driving John crazy. They kept finding adjustments for John to record in the accounting records. Apparently, many of the methods he used to capture transactions in the accounting system did not comply with required accounting practices. John thought they were being rather picky about some of the issues. The auditors questioned his method of recording purchases, subscription revenues, advertising expenses, and charge-backs on credit cards, just to name a few of their concerns.

The biggest issue involved John's accounting for the costs of purchasing movies. This issue first came to light when *MoviesDoorToDoor.com* obtained the loan for the server. At that point, Meredith questioned the method John was using to reflect those costs in the accounting and tax records. He was recording the costs of movie purchases as expenses in the "Movie Costs" category. However, based on his discussions with Meredith and Courtney's reading of her accounting textbook, John agreed to reclassify all costs in the "Movie Costs" expense category to the Balance Sheet as an asset. So, after the loan was closed, John spent several hours correcting their accounting records to reflect movie purchases as an asset.

Once those costs were on the Balance Sheet as an asset, Courtney explained that those costs needed to be gradually expensed as depreciation over their estimated useful lives. Courtney showed John how to calculate depreciation using the straight-line method of depreciation, which wasn't too complicated. She and John estimated that the useful life of a typical video or DVD was about three years. Based on that, John began depreciating those costs over the remaining part of the estimated useful lives.

The problem raised by the auditor wasn't related to reflecting the movie costs as an asset. As a matter of fact, the auditors agreed the account classification was appropriate. Instead, the auditors disagreed with Courtney and John's estimate of the useful lives for videos and DVDs. The auditors believed that the three year estimate wasn't reasonable, explaining that the industry trend was to depreciate those costs over a much shorter estimated life equal to one year. They pointed to a recent article in *The Wall Street Journal* discussing the write-down of movie costs by one of the larger video rental chains after revising its estimated useful life for videos to nine months! The auditors seemed to be quite firm in their belief that *MoviesDoorToDoor.com's* estimate of the useful life needed to be shortened to reflect the industry trend.

That news really frustrated John. He had spent so much time correcting the financial statements after Meredith's concerns were highlighted. Now he was going to have to redo all the accounting records again. Additionally, John felt like the estimate suggested by the auditor didn't make sense, as many of their movies had been on their shelves for well beyond a year. Any excess copies of movies not frequently rented were quickly sold by *MoviesDoorToDoor.com.*

The auditors argued that because the typical rental value of a movie is greatest in its release year, there wasn't much of a useful rental life once other more current movies arrived. So, they believed a one year useful life was appropriate, as the rental value was negligible beyond one year.

John countered their arguments by pointing out how *MoviesDoorTo-Door.com's* business strategy of using its movie search engine to suggest alternative movies for customers to watch actually resulted in higher rental rates for older movies. John was trying anything to keep from having to correct his accounting records.

John kept Brad and Courtney updated on the issue; however despite his complaining, Brad and Courtney kept trying to get John to lighten up. They felt like it was more important to be consistent with the policy of the national chain, and they didn't think the adjustments needed would significantly affect the purchase price.

After an extensive debate, John and the auditors finally agreed to use an estimated useful life of one and one-half years. The auditors also agreed to help John calculate the necessary adjustment to the records.

Once that issue was settled, it took the auditors another week or so to complete the audit. Everyone was anxious to see that occur, since the financial statements would influence the purchase price.

The national chain's market research and the audited financial statements eventually led to a purchase price offer of $5.5 million dollars. The offer assumed that Brad, Courtney, and John would continue as employees of the national chain for a period of three years.

While the threesome was comfortable with the purchase price, there were concerns about continuing with the business as employees. The hard feelings generated from the "sweat equity" share allocation made the thought of continuing to work together hard to accept. Brad's immediate response was, "No way! I want out of this business."

Courtney hated hearing Brad say that. She felt like John's recent behavior continued to fuel Brad's resentment. She kept wanting to put the share allocation issue behind them, but John's constant complaining about the unfair allocation kept pouring salt on the wound. Courtney couldn't understand why John couldn't get over this issue, since in the end all three of them would be more wealthy than they ever dreamed.

As Courtney thought about the offer over the next few days, she was beginning to wonder if she wanted to continue working at *MoviesDoorTo-Door.com* as well. She was really starting to doubt her relationship with John. A few days later, Courtney shocked John when she finally declared, "I'm not sure I want to continue working here either."

"What do you mean, Courtney?" asked John. "I'm not surprised by Brad's decision to pull out, but I didn't expect this from you. I thought we were partners both inside and outside of work."

"You sure have a funny way of showing it," responded Courtney. "All I see you doing is work. You haven't made any effort to spend time with me. As a matter of fact, Steve has made more of an effort to spend time with me over the last few months than you."

"What are you talking about?" asked John.

"See, this is what I'm talking about," explained Courtney. "You haven't been paying enough attention to me to realize how often I've seen Steve. I've spent more time outside of work with him than you, lately."

"Are you telling me that you're dating Steve?" asked John.

"No. I wouldn't call it that," answered Courtney. "But my time with him has made me realize that I want more out of a relationship than you're able to provide." After a short pause, she went on to say, "I need to get away for a while to think about our future together."

"You realize that your unwillingness to continue working with the national chain will impact the purchase price," said John. "Remember, their offer drops to $3.9 million if none of us is willing to continue working after the purchase. So, the decisions of Brad and you will cost us all dearly."

"John, you can continue working for them," responded Courtney. "The company seems to be all you care about anyway."

"Well, I'm going to continue working with them," said John. "And, if you and Brad don't, I expect to receive a higher pay-out from the purchase than you."

"John, enough is enough," responded Courtney. "You're not getting a higher pay-out than either of us. Remember, Brad and I have the controlling majority vote, and we'll never go for it. If you think you deserve more, then start negotiating a higher salary to be paid by the national chain once you're an employee."

"Your behavior is making me wonder if I want to continue in a relationship with you as well," responded John in frustration. "I can't believe you're letting your emotions get the best of you."

"Obviously, this conversation is digressing," said Courtney. "Since you want to be the one who continues working for the national chain, you need to talk with them about how the offer would change with Brad and me not staying on board."

"Are you sure Brad isn't going to continue?" asked John.

"Yes. I just talked with him before meeting with you," said Courtney. "He's definitely out. Unfortunately you haven't helped the situation over the last few months. Your behavior has confirmed in his mind that he doesn't want to work with you anymore. In fact, he's moving to Austin once the deal is completed."

"Fine. I'll survive on my own," said John. "I'm going to call the national chain to explain the situation and have them work on a counter-proposal."

"When you do, be sure to tell them that Brad and I will take nothing less than $4.4 million," explained Courtney. "You can negotiate more, if you want. But, just know we're willing to settle for that amount."

* * * * *

When John went back to the national chain, he started his negotiation at $4.9 million, with the understanding that he would be the only one continuing after the purchase. The reaction by senior management of the national chain was somewhat reserved. However, after some discussion the national chain became more comfortable once they realized John was the main person handling the technical aspects of the movie search engine. The national chain believed they could find people to help provide the movie description content. They were most concerned about having someone with the technical expertise to keep the web search engine functioning. John could provide that.

After several iterations between John and the national chain, they finally agreed to a purchase price of $4.7 million, assuming John would continue to work for a period of three years. When John shared the news with Brad and Courtney, they were ready to sign the documents immediately. Both Brad and Courtney were growing more eager to move on. They believed that they would make enough money on the deal to cover them for a life-time. So, they didn't want to negotiate further. They pushed John to get the deal completed as soon as possible.

John decided to update his mother about the negotiations before responding officially to the offer. She was pleased with the negotiated purchase price for both John and her. Because her investment had turned out far better than ever anticipated, she agreed they should go forward with accepting the offer.

Based on the reactions of all stockholders, John proceeded to finalize the buyout with the national chain.

* * * * *

Brad, Courtney and John all had mixed emotions when they finally met at the lawyer's office to close the deal. They hadn't spoken much to each other since the day they agreed to the purchase price terms. While each was amazed that their Friday night dream over three years ago had blossomed to $4.7 million so quickly, they all entered the room with an empty feeling because of the way their friendship appeared to be dissolving.

Courtney was having flashbacks to when they all first joined Interconnectivity. She clearly recounted the Friday night they came up with the business idea. How thankful she was that Brad and John continued to push the idea, even though she initially thought it was crazy. Courtney especially had favorable memories of the early days when she worked closely with John on the development of the movie search engine.

Now, Courtney was finding it hard to believe that the three of them were becoming so detached after all the excitement and fun they had developing the business. She particularly couldn't stop thinking about her relationship with John, which appeared to be fizzling. At times she wondered if her initial gut reaction of John when she first met him at Interconnectivity was on target. He appeared to be self-absorbed then and still seemed to be that way now. However, while certain aspects of John were annoying, she recognized he could be loads of fun whenever she could capture his attention. The more she thought about it, their relationship had actually been progressing up until Steve reappeared in Raleigh and the national chain approached them about the buyout.

All this was now confusing Courtney. She didn't know what to do and wanted to escape from Raleigh for a while to clear her mind. Fortunately, her sister was willing to go on a week-long cruise with her. Courtney swore she wouldn't decide what to do next until she was back.

The finality of the situation was also starting to hit John. He was beginning to focus on the fact that he wouldn't see Courtney's smile everyday at work. And, he was beginning to realize he had neglected his relationship with her. His philosophy had always been to work hard now so he could reap the benefits later. In the end, it was becoming more clear to John that this philosophy was getting in the way of his relationship with Courtney. While he had convinced himself that Courtney understood the importance of their working hard now so they could enjoy each other later, he now recognized that wasn't the case. Courtney needed to spend more personal time with him than he had made possible.

John really wanted to talk with Courtney about their future. But, it was clear she wasn't ready or willing to talk. He would probably need to give her some space for a while and not push the issue until she was ready. But, John hated to be in a position of just waiting and hoping for the best. The feeling of having things out of his control was uncomfortable.

Brad felt the least remorse about the breakup of the three friends and wasn't concerned about what would be next in his life. He knew that John would never try to reconcile with him over the disagreements about the share allocation and buyout. While he knew John was self-centered, he never dreamed that John could be so greedy. It was going to take a lot of time to get that thought out of his mind.

Very few thoughts of the early days ran through Brad's mind. Instead, he was more focused on his new life in Austin where he would be spending a lot more time with Maggie. She was the special companion he wanted for a lifetime. And, on top of that, his new found wealth was going to allow him to pursue his literary dream of writing a novel. The experiences of the past few years with *MoviesDoorToDoor.com* would provide substantial content for his story. And, Brad had already found a lake house in the hill country near Maggie's parents. He looked forward to the beauty and serenity of the lake. He was beginning to wonder, "How much better could it be?"

The only remorse Brad felt was when Courtney gave him a hug and indicated that she would miss him. That brought back fond memories of their friendship. He realized that their lives had been intertwined ever since they first met at Interconnectivity. He would miss having Courtney as a confidant. She was a great listener and showed so much compassion, particularly as his relationship with Maggie developed. But the reality now was they were into different seasons of their lives.

Silence fell over the room once all the documents were signed and arrangements for the transfer of funds to all the *MoviesDoorToDoor.com* stockholders were set. The process of signing the documents had diverted their attention temporarily. But now, the reality that this chapter of their lives was about to be end hit them hard. While each knew their financial success was far beyond their expectations, they all realized there had been major personal costs. They stood to leave, all wondering what would become of their friendship. As Brad reached to open the conference room door, he paused for a moment, turned to face Courtney and John, and said, "Let me treat you guys to lunch."

Discussion Questions

1. Why do companies seek to acquire other entities?

2. Why do you think the national chain sought to acquire *MoviesDoorToDoor.com*?

3. What kinds of factors would be considered by the national chain as they determined the purchase price for the acquisition of *MoviesDoorToDoor.com*?

4. Why would the national chain be willing to pay *MoviesDoorToDoor.com* stockholders $4.7 million, an amount far exceeding the fair market value of the acquired assets?

5. Calculate how much Brad, Courtney, and John each received based on their respective ownership percentages.

6. What does the difference between the purchase price of $4.7 million and the aggregate fair market value of the acquired net assets represent on the national chain's financial statements?

7. When the national chain records the purchase transaction in their accounting records, what financial statement accounts would be affected?

8. How would the difference described in question #6 above be accounted for by the national chain in years after the purchase?

9. What factors might impact a company's decision to use different estimates of useful lives for property, plant, and equipment relative to other entities in the industry?

10. What depreciation method might be appropriate if the economic value of a depreciable asset declines more in the early years than in later years?

11. John's mom purchased 3,600 shares at a price of $5.00 per share. The national chain ultimately paid $4.7 million to acquire all 78,000 of the outstanding shares. Show your calculations of the price the national chain paid per share. Assume that his mom held those shares for exactly 3 years, what average annual compounded return did she earn on her investment?

12. The national chain paid cash for the entire purchase price. Often companies acquire other entities by exchanging their stock. What are the advantages of acquiring a company by issuing stock rather than by paying cash?

13. What would you do next if you were in Brad, Courtney, or John's shoes?